The POWER *of*
MONEY

Books by Kenneth Ulmer

The Champion in You

Available from Destiny Image Publishers

The POWER *of* MONEY

How to AVOID *a* DEVIL'S SNARE

Kenneth C. Ulmer

DESTINY IMAGE® PUBLISHERS, INC.

P.O. Box 310, Shippensburg, PA 17257-0310

"Speaking to the Purposes of God for This Generation and for the Generations to Come."

This book and all other Destiny Image, Revival Press, MercyPlace, Fresh Bread, Destiny Image Fiction, and Treasure House books are available at Christian bookstores and distributors worldwide.

For a U.S. bookstore nearest you, call **1-800-722-6774**.

For more information on foreign distributors, call **717-532-3040**.

Reach us on the Internet: **www.destinyimage.com**.

ISBN 10: 0-7684-3199-9

ISBN 13: 978-0-7684-3199-5

For Worldwide Distribution, Printed in the U.S.A.

1 2 3 4 5 6 7 8 9 10 11 / 13 12 11 10

COMMENTS ON THE WRITINGS OF KENNETH C. ULMER

Ken Ulmer is one of America's new voices, rising with a penetrating call to pragmatic spiritual dynamics. As a Christian leader, he stands tall; as a servant to society, he stands out; as a friend, he stands trustworthy; as a man of God, he stands close—in touch with our Father, that he might be in touch with Him whose touch can change the world. Knowing Dr. Ulmer as I do, I attest to this: the man is real to the core! The truths with which he inspires multitudes becomes real and livable because he is relating what he's learned and lived and proven.

—Jack W. Hayford
President, Foursquare Churches International
Chancellor, The King's College and Seminary
Founding Pastor, The Church On The Way

Bishop Kenneth Ulmer reveals from Scripture just how completely and fantastically our great God and Savior loves and cares for us, illuminating facets of His being that many believers have no doubt never considered.

—The Late Dr. Bill Bright
Founder of Campus Crusade for Christ

Dr. Ulmer is one of the most strategic Christian leaders in the nation. His impact in helping people understand God's principles for life is enriching while remaining biblical. It is hard to overstate the impact Dr. Ulmer makes on tens of thousands of Christians every week.

—Dr. Mark Brewer
Senior Pastor
Bel Air Presbyterian Church, Los Angeles

Dr. Ken Ulmer does what he does best. He slices through the confusion, misunderstanding, and misinformation and then clearly and accurately explains the Scripture.

—Robert Morris
Best selling Author, *The Blessed Life*

The Power of Money: How to Avoid a Devil's Snare

Such a balanced Biblical teaching! This is a topic that too many preachers today teach as a "name it and claim it and blab it and grab it" theology. Bishop Ulmer has great wisdom and insight on the subject of Mammon.

—Pastor Benny Hinn (as quoted on *This is Your Day*)

The Champion in You

In a world that is filled with so many people who feel defeated or fearful, this word comes at a needy time. Bishop Kenneth Ulmer shares insights that transform the reader from the dismal to the dynamic. Take a read and watch the truths transform you until you emerge undaunted—a champion for Christ!

—Bishop T.D. Jakes Sr.
The Potter's House of Dallas, Inc.

My prayer is that, as you read *The Champion in You*, God would stir in your heart that you would be a champion in your generation. We need men and women to stand up and champion the cause of God in our world. God has great things for you and you are a champion in Him!

—John Bevere
Author and Speaker
Cofounder, Messenger International
Colorado Springs/Australia/United Kingdom

This book will unlock what God has destined each of us to be, and that is a champion. This isn't some quick fix, gimmick-filled book. Bishop Ulmer gives practical biblical principles that will inform you and help you to lead a transformed and empowered life. This book will change your life.

—Bishop Noel Jones

This is a very exciting book! It is a can't-put-it-down page-turner by one of today's most inspiring communicators. In *The Champion in You*, Kenneth Ulmer vividly portrays a divinely inspired, powerful biblical truth: God has placed within each of us a champion waiting to be discovered and released to be used for His glory and the encouragement of all those around us. If you want to get acquainted with this champion in you, this book will show you the way!

—Dr. Lloyd Ogilvie
Former Chaplin, U.S. Senate

Making Your Money Count

Pick up this book and prepare to be changed!...[Dr. Ulmer] clearly articulates biblically sound truth on the topic of money. ...Ulmer brings us back to what the Bible really has to say on money and how we should use what we have.

—John Bevere
Author and Speaker
Cofounder, Messenger International
Colorado Springs/Australia/United Kingdom

This book is astounding...Ulmer counters the critics' questions of whether God wants us to be rich with solid, fundamental truths found throughout the Bible.

—Bishop Eddie L. Long
New Birth Baptist Church; Atlanta, Georgia

It's a special delight to commend this evenhanded, insightful, and practical tool that untwists a subject that's too often mangled by poor exposition or distorted by exaggeration....[It is] a solid resource from a leader who provides us with the whole package: a book written by a wise pastor, a balanced teacher, a thorough-going scholar, a Bible-preacher, and a passionate and godly man. Through *Making Your Money Count,* stewarding our finances is made alive and done right!"

—Jack W. Hayford
President, Foursquare Churches International
Chancellor, The King's College and Seminary
Founding Pastor, The Church On The Way

I would urge anyone who wants to know God's process for lifting people from poverty to financial productivity and wise money management to read this book! If you deal with money—whether you are rich, poor, or in between—this book is for you. If you want to learn how to ease your monetary struggles...and help others who may be struggling financially, this book shows you how. It contains new thinking on a psychological and biblical foundation that I applaud.

—Dr. Robert H. Schuller
Crystal Cathedral, California

...A benchmark book by a dynamic scholar preacher that is inspiring and instructive....In this powerful and penetrating book, Bishop Ulmer plumbs the depths of the biblical meaning of prosperity. He confronts the false teaching of both the divine right presumption and the anti-prosperity predispositions in contemporary Christianity. ...Ulmer is one of the truly great spiritual leaders of our time.

—Dr. Lloyd Ogilvie
Former Chaplin, U.S. Senate

…Among all the parables in the Bible, two-thirds speak to the issue of money. We all grapple with the question of how to be good stewards of our resources. What a blessing it is that Bishop Kenneth Ulmer has written a practical guide on the subject based on God's Word. Thank you, Bishop!

—Angela Bassett and Courtney B. Vance

In His Image

My dear friend, Bishop Kenneth Ulmer, is one of the most outstanding, creative preachers of our time. With *In His Image,* he has given us creative biblical treasure that will not only capture our minds, but will also move our hearts toward a God whose heart is moved toward us. Reading this book will compel you to love God more deeply and to worship Him more fully!

—Dr. Crawford W. Loritts, Jr.
Author, Radio Host
Associate Director, Campus Crusade for Christ

CONTENTS

INTRODUCTION

HAVE you have ever felt as though you've tried your very best to serve God, to live for Him, to do things His way, yet, in spite of your desire, sincerity, and efforts, it seems as though your financial affairs are in a perpetual state of struggle? A struggle to maintain "break even." A struggle to get ahead. A struggle to keep your spending in perspective with your priorities.

You love the Lord and you know you're not perfect. You also know you're doing your absolute best and, still, getting from paycheck to paycheck *and* being able to save a little for a rainy day is a *struggle*. You're not trying to be overly spiritual and say that because you love the Lord you shouldn't have money problems, but there are times when you think, *Something is not working here. What am I doing wrong?*

You are not alone. There are tens of thousands of people who are also doing their best from day to day. They, too, find it hard to understand why they're barely keeping their financial heads above water. They wonder why things are in such a state of perpetually precarious balance.

It seems that every Christian, in the desire to love and serve the Lord and to walk in His ways, has, at any given point in life, been subjected to a fierce struggle involving money. The bad news is that, as we will learn about in this book, there is a specific force at work behind the scenes that is responsible for keeping us in fear and worry in the area of our monetary affairs. The good news is that *there is a solution*. There is a way to nullify the effects of this constant struggle over finances.

Financial Freedom Begins With Worship

The next time the topic of finances comes up between you and your spouse, notice how the atmosphere changes. An attitude creeps in. Necks start rolling. Eyebrows rise. Heads wag back and forth. A particular tone of voice takes over.

Not long ago during a trip to the Ukraine, my wife and I were having a wonderful discussion. We were feeling great. We were saying to each other, "Praise the Lord! It's so nice to be here. Are you having a good time, honey?" All those lovey-dovey feelings people in love express when they're happy.

Then, I said something that had a dollar sign somehow connected to it. For the life of me, I do not recall exactly what I said, but it had something to do with money, and—I am not kidding you—you would have thought a cold north wind blew in. It was like somebody rang a bell and my wife went to her corner and I went to mine. We squared off...and went straight into the twilight zone.

After dinner I said to her, "Sweetheart, did you *see that?* Something weird happened back there."

She agreed that something strange had come between us. We got into a lengthy discussion about how the whole climate had changed—how the sweet talk vanished, lips began to curl, eyes rolled, and attitudes set in.

How is it that relationships can be so joyous and happy and fun, but when you talk about money, the atmosphere changes and a struggle ensues—even in the best of relationships? The answer isn't terribly complex, but it does require a bit of study. Surprisingly, the answer begins with *worship.*

We're going to examine this topic very carefully, and with at least two good reasons: First, the information is life-impacting for those who want to understand the critical importance of walking in God's ways. Second, it reveals a force whose mission it is to divert us from that very purpose. Indeed, it is an entity who has very cleverly and successfully duped virtually every human being on planet Earth—Christians included.

Before we begin our study of what causes so many of us to feel the grip of continual challenges related to money, material possessions, wealth, riches, and financial matters in general, I want to lay some important groundwork. Bear with me for a few pages; what I have to say might not at first seem connected with breaking the grip of financial struggle. But it is actually at the very heart of understanding this phenomenon.

The Spirit of Worship

On a recent travel itinerary I preached at a church in Cape Town, South Africa, where blacks, whites, and Indians were gathered together in one church. Twenty years ago, that would have been unheard of. Even ten years ago, it would have been extremely rare. Young people sang and ministered and blessed the congregation; right there in Cape Town, people of all different ethnicities worshiped with one another.

I left that church and went to Johannesburg. It was a Saturday morning. Thousands of pastors and leaders were gathered in a hall where we danced and celebrated and worshiped together.

The next day, I went to Rhema Church, the largest church in South Africa. It is a mostly black congregation whose pastor is my dear friend and a great man of God, Ray McCaulley, a white man. We all worshiped together, under the leadership of a Caucasian—something that would have been unimaginable in Africa, even into the 1990s.

From Rhema I went to the World Pentecostal Conference, where nearly 50 countries were represented by more than 40 different churches. There, we all celebrated the power of God under the anointing of the Holy Spirit and in the flow of the Spirit and the Word of God. It was a move that had its genesis decades earlier in downtown Los Angeles with a one-eyed black ex-Baptist preacher by the name of W.J. Seymour.

That same spirit of unity and worship together through the Holy Ghost that began with Pastor Seymour had by now spread all around the world. And there at that World Pentecostal Conference, tens of thousands of people worshiped together.

After the conference, I went into one of the South African townships, where 14 groups of pastors from over a dozen different denominations (none of whom had ever worshiped together before) were now worshiping. They all loved Jesus and were saved, sanctified, purchased by His blood, and filled with the Holy Ghost. Yet, they had never come together in one place to worship with one another. For two nights, we worshiped there. It was glorious.

The following Sunday, I traveled to London, to a suburb called Brompton where I went to Holy Trinity church, a charismatic Anglican congregation. I sat in the very back. I wasn't wearing a cross or my collar. Nobody knew me. It was a wonderful feeling being at Holy Trinity in that racially mixed group. There were Asians, Nigerians, Caucasians, Islanders. All of us were under the power of the Holy Spirit, and we worshiped in unity.

I left Brompton and went to Kiev, to a conference hosted by the largest church in Europe. More than 4,000 pastors and leaders from nearly three dozen countries were gathered there. Most of the pastors in attendance didn't speak a word of English. My sermon had to be translated into Ukrainian.

The fervor of the dance, worship, and praise to God was stunning. The pastor was a Black man from Nigeria, my friend and brother Sunday Adalaja, whose church was 99 percent Caucasian. And we all worshiped together!

Worship is the only part of gatherings of believers where God is the object. Worship is powerful. It breaks down walls. It releases grips of oppression, sadness, anger, envy—those human emotions that overtake us from time to time and can be so destructive in our lives. Even the devil knows the potential effects of the power of worship. It is so potent that the *only* thing satan asked Jesus to give him when he took Him up on the high mountain and offered Him all of the riches of the world was *worship* (see Matt. 4:8-9; Luke 4:5-7).

Misplaced worship, however, can have disastrous effects. This is true whether or not we realize that we are directing our worship at the wrong object.

Consider the story from John 4:3-26, about the Samaritan woman Jesus met at the well.

Jesus is on His way from Judea to Galilee when He stops at Jacob's well, just outside of Samaria. As He sits there, resting from His journey, a woman comes to the well to draw water. Other than the fact that she is from Samaria, the woman is not named (which means that you can put your name in the story).

Jesus asks her for a favor, saying, "Give Me a drink of water."

To paraphrase the story, He and the woman then got into a discussion in which Jesus easily and quickly transitions from talking about natural water to "spiritual water."

The woman responds, "You don't even have a bucket to draw water with."

Jesus replies, "I've got some water for you that, if you drink it, you will never thirst again. It will become in you like a fountain springing up to everlasting life."

She says, in essence, "I'll take it."

But Jesus ignores her request and, oddly, changes the subject. He says, "Go call your husband."

What in the world is the connection between worship and Jesus telling the woman to go call her husband? Jesus began to zero in on that very connection.

The woman hems and haws a little bit and finally says, "I'm not married. I don't have a husband."

"You got that right," Jesus responds. "You've had five husbands. And now you're living with somebody you're not married to." She was shacking up!

The woman then does as many of us do when we're directly confronted by the Word and the will of God—she changes the subject: "I perceive that you are a prophet, oh man of God." With that attempt to *get deep*, the woman has played right into the Master's hand. She continues, "My people *worship* in this mountain. You're a Jew. You *worship* on another mountain." And with that response, she steps right into His purpose for entering her life that day.

Jesus responds, "You worship what you do not know." He tells her that the time is coming, and has already arrived, when worship will not be about where, but about *whom*. He says to her, "God is Spirit. Those who worship Him must worship Him *in spirit and in truth*. The Father is seeking such to worship Him."

What He is telling the woman is that up until that point, people had been worshiping their things their way, but they had been *worshiping the wrong things*—without even realizing it. They had been duped.

As the exchange between Jesus and the woman at the well reveals, God is looking for *something specific.* He's on a mission. He is not seeking people who are spiritually "deep." He's not even seeking church people. He's seeking worshipers who will recognize who He is and will make a determination to worship Him in spirit and in truth. What Jesus is saying is that true worship is always the synthesis and balance of spirit and truth. It isn't spirit *or* truth; it is spirit *and* truth.

Worshipers of God must worship Him in spirit and in truth. The word *in* has two connotations. First, it is a word having to do with location. Second, it is a word involving instrumentality. Worshipers of the true God (who is Spirit) must worship Him in location—that is, in the sphere, context, and dimension of the Spirit. This means that in the process of worshiping God, a shift occurs between what we do in the flesh and what is impacted in the spirit realm. It means that true worship of our Maker *goes beyond what we do in the flesh.* Worship that proceeds from a skewed motivation (whether intentional or from a lack of understanding of the forces involved) can actually be a conduit to worshiping *what we never intended to worship.* Therefore, it can hinder or even prevent the worship of God.

There are some things that God wants to put in order in His house, things He wants to put into place, things God wants to shift and change. He wants to stretch us and grow us and take us beyond where we are now, past our current understanding (see 2 Pet. 3:18) of His realm and past the grip of forces that seek to twist our understanding of how His realm (His Kingdom) operates.

God wants this from us because we don't serve a mediocre God. Therefore, we are not to be a mediocre people. We're not called to be an ordinary church or a usual ministry. We are not average; we are beyond average because our Father is a God who has placed a calling on each one of our lives. That calling is to take us beyond the status quo, beyond the way we are now.

He wants us to begin thinking and operating at a higher level. His desire is that we would see through the lens of His Word how economic processes function here on earth and understand how they contrast with His ways and His model (see

Isa. 55:8-9). This would enable us to shed the worldly way of thinking that keeps so many of us in the grip of financial struggle. To do this requires a renewing of the mind, a fresh way of looking at how God wants us to operate.

It is imperative that we gain understanding of the insidious influences exerted against us by a powerful opponent who stands against God's methods and whose sole mission is to twist our thinking about the truth regarding money, riches, finances, and material possessions.

Breaking What Hinders

This understanding begins when we focus our worship on the Creator of the world—the one thing above all else that the devil does not want us to do—and that is the key. Remember, when the devil had his one shot at going face-to-face with Jesus in the flesh here on Earth, his one chance to try to win it all before Jesus even began His ministry, all satan wanted from Jesus in exchange for *every material thing* on the planet was the one thing he knew was key to ruling the world: **worship**.

Even the devil knows the invincible power of worship. Even he knows that *worship is the key to everything*. And yet, these days, the only part of a church service that is exclusively and specifically directed *to* God is the praise and worship time at the beginning of the service. Makes you wonder why it's called *service*. Whom are we serving? Every element of the church service after the first 10 or 20 minutes of praise and worship is all *about* God, *about* His Word, *about* things related to God.

Here's a news flash: *It is more important to worship God than to talk about God.* Don't get me wrong; it is crucially important that we learn about God and His Word. However, of the standard 60- or 90-minute church service today, 75 to 85 percent of what goes on is directed to *us* and not to God.

Sadly, church has become mostly about us. Too many come to church with the attitude of *I come to get a word.* How selfish! We are to *give* praise to God. We are to *give* worship to God. We are to *give* honor to God. We are to *give* glory to God. We are to *give* reverence to God. To come to church mostly to *get* is to dishonor the very God who gave us the power to get whatever it is we're going to receive during our lives.

We need to keep in mind why the devil was thrust like lightning out of the presence of God (see Luke 10:18): it was because he wanted God to worship him, which was why he offered Christ all of the riches of the world for it (see Luke 4:7).

God does not want us to be a self-focused people. He wants us to realize that all we have comes from a God who is our source, the one in whom we live and move and have our being (see Acts 17:28). There is nothing and nobody else that is to be worshiped on earth but God.

Our getting away from the pure worship of God—the "in spirit and in truth" kind of worship—is at the core of a frightening reality of which most of us are unaware. Over the millennia, this reality has overtaken virtually all understanding of how God wants us to think and to operate in the one area of our lives that is at the root of more fractured relationships than any other, including our relationship with God Himself.

Many of us are actually worshiping something other than God because we have been taught to do so by a particular system, a skewed methodology, a false mind-set manufactured outside the will of God. This way of thinking is one that most of us have been operating under all of our lives without even realizing it—a mind-set that even the Church often helps to perpetuate.

In this book, I am going to "unpack" the truth of a topic that is rarely discussed (or even taught) in churches today: the existence of a specific force that has obtained an insidious grip on the way we view money, riches, finances, and material possessions. If we don't stop allowing a force like that to manipulate these four areas of our lives, we put ourselves in danger of continuing to live under the delusion that we are fighting the good fight of faith, when we're actually living life trapped in a devil's snare.

Chapter One

THE INTRIGUING CHALLENGE OF REAL WORSHIP

REAL worship of God is a central key to sleuthing out the source of a massive and clever deception behind how most people (Christians and non-Christians alike) have been taught to view finances, money, material blessings, and possessions. One of the things that prevents us from pursuing God with our worship is that we focus on ourselves and on what *we* are getting, rather than on God.

After a church service, for example, some people grumble, "I didn't get much from the service today." Well, maybe you didn't bring much today—no words of praise to God, no attitude of worship to God. Yet God blessed you with another week on the job He provided; and He gave you the mind, strength, and ability to serve on that job. The truth is, He alone has been your source and has provided all of your needs.

He more than deserves our worship in truth, which means to worship Him truth-*fully*, in the full truth of who He is in our lives and the role He alone wants to play in *blessing* us.

Surprisingly, one of the intriguing challenges to worshiping God in full truth happens to be the Church herself. The Church has become, in many instances, a skilled hypocrite, though perhaps unwittingly. For example, in many churches today, you have to walk in line or you're out of line. You hear this exchange in thousands of churches around the world every Sunday:

"Good morning, brother."

"Praise the Lord, sister. Praise the Lord!"

"How are you today?"

"I'm great. Things are *wonderful.*" Meanwhile, what this brother is thinking is a different story altogether: *Do you really want to know how I am? Truth is, this has been a heck of a trying week. Bills are being paid late—if at all. My paycheck is being spread thinner than butter across burnt toast. No, things are not so wonderful.*

There are churches where you can't admit realities like this. If you do admit that you're going through a rough patch, you are making a "negative confession." But you're not being negative at all; you're simply telling the truth. You're experiencing some challenges. There are some hurdles you can't seem to get behind you right now; that's all. You still love Jesus. He still loves you. You're still going to Heaven. You just had a tough week.

It's all right to be honest with people about how things are going. This should be especially true with our fellow Christians, who will then know what to pray for us. Tell the truth. "I'm going through some struggles." It doesn't have to be with a whining or defeatist attitude; just a statement of the facts for today.

I have difficulty relating to people who say they love Jesus and imply that they have never been through struggles. How do you know what God can do if you've never been through something so He can show you what He can do to lift you out of it? Why do you even need Him if you never really *need* Him? How do you know you're a champion if you've never been through a battle? How do you know you're a winner if you've never been in a struggle?

"In this world," Jesus said in John 16:33, *"you will have trouble"* (NIV). He wasn't giving a negative confession. He was just stating the truth. Here is the truth that God wants us to get: He wants our worship, and He wants us to worship Him in spirit and in truth (see John 4:24). This is the key to getting through struggles with the attitude of Christ. Cool, calm, and in command.

The process of peeling back the layers of biblical teaching related to understanding and breaking the grip of financial struggles begins with an incident from the life of Jesus: when the devil took Him up on the high mountain at the start of His public ministry on earth:

> *Then the devil, taking Him up on a high mountain, showed Him all the kingdoms of the world in a moment of time. And the devil said to Him, "All this authority I will give You, and their glory; for this has been delivered to me, and I give it to whomever I wish. Therefore, if You will worship before me, all will be Yours" (Luke 4:5-7).*

In this passage, the devil takes Jesus to a high mountain in the desert and shows Him all the riches of the world in the twinkling of an eye—*bam!*—shows Him everything, saying, "All this is Yours if You will worship me."

It's important to understand the significance of what is happening: It's Jesus and the devil, one on one. The word *worship* is in an interesting Greek tense known as *aorist*, which indicates something that is done in a moment of time. The devil is saying, "I'll give you all of this if you'll worship me *just one time.*"

The Greek word for *worship* is *proskuneo*, which means "to bow before, to kneel before, to crouch before." It is the same word that might be used, for example, of a dog who laps at the foot of his master or licks the hand of his owner; "to fawn... or prostrate oneself in homage."[1] The devil is saying, "If you'll get on Your knees and bow down at my feet just one time, this is all Yours. Nobody's here but You and me. I won't tell anyone. You only have to do it one time and I'll give You all the kingdoms of the world."[2]

Jesus responded to the devil by quoting from Deuteronomy 6:13, as Luke 4:8 records: *"Get behind Me, Satan! For it is written, 'You shall worship the Lord your God, and Him only you shall serve.'"*

This exchange tells us two things God wants from us: He wants our worship and He wants our service. He says, in essence, "The truth is, you shall only worship the Lord your God, and Him only shall you serve." We are to worship God only, because He is the only truth (see John 14:6); and we are to serve Him only, because only He is God.

Then, in John 4:23, Jesus told the woman at the well *how* to worship God: *"The hour is coming, and now is, when the true worshipers will worship the Father **in spirit and truth**...."*

Why will the true worshipers worship God in spirit and truth? Because God commands us, in Deuteronomy 6:13, to worship and serve Him only. Jesus adds, in John 4:24, that those who worship God must worship Him in spirit and truth; and in John 14:15, He notes that those who love God will obey Him. Thus, true worshipers (those who love God and desire to obey Him) will worship God as He instructs them to.

So far, we have learned three things:

1. God wants our worship.

2. God wants our service.

3. God wants our worship to be in spirit and in truth.

The Rival God Named *Mammon*

Now go to Matthew 6:24, a verse located in the middle of the Sermon on the Mount, which contains Jesus' teachings on the ethical principles of the Kingdom of God:

> *No one can serve two masters; for either he will hate the one and love the other, or else he will be loyal to the one and despise the other. You cannot serve God and mammon* (Matthew 6:24).

In this verse, we learn that God wants our motivation to serve Him to be based in two things:

1. He wants us to serve Him out of *love*.

2. He wants us to serve Him out of *loyalty*.

God says you cannot serve two masters, because you will hate one and love the other (and He wants to be loved). Or, you will turn from the one and be loyal to the other (and He wants your loyalty).

Then Jesus added, *"You cannot serve God and mammon."* Some Bible versions say "God and wealth"; some say "God and worldly riches"; and some say, "God and Money."

The translation "Money" raises an interesting issue. Money, in and of itself, is an inanimate object, a thing. God is alive. Comparing the two would be incongruent; You can't *serve* a live God and a dead thing. Money has neither volition nor will; money is amoral.

If Jesus' instruction about whom to serve was purely a choice between God and inanimate money, He would have told us to stay as far away from money as possible. Period. Instead, money is one of the ways God blesses us. Logically speaking, the context of the Lord's instruction indicates that He was referring to more than mere money. The only solution to this seemingly incongruous comparison is that Jesus was presenting a choice between two *like* entities.

We already know that God is a viable being, a live Person. Could it be that Jesus was telling us that the entity referred to as *money* or *mammon* in Matthew 6:24 is also alive?

What was Jesus trying to warn us about? Let's go to the Greek. The Greek for "mammon" is *mamonas*. One key translation of this word is "wealth personified."[3] This indicates that the word refers not to a thing, but a being—a person. At least one major translation of the Bible, the New International Version, translates the original Greek *mamonas* to the English word, *Money*, capitalizing it as you would a proper name. Again, this indicates a live entity—a person. It is clear: In His warning, Jesus was referring to God and another person.

The word *Mammon* is the name, not for money (the "thing") but for an actual, tangible god who is the power and the demonic influence behind money. Webster's Dictionary also defines *Mammon* as "wealth...more or less personified."[4] Again, the revelation is clear: the "Mammon" Jesus talks about in Matthew 6:24 refers to *an actual being* who is somehow attached to "wealth" (the definition of which we will discuss in the following chapter).

Now the comparison in the verse makes sense: it is a discussion of two living entities: God and a live being referred to by the name of *Money* or *Mammon*. God is saying that you cannot worship Him as your Master and Mammon as your master. The choice is distinct; it is between one who is the true God and one who is a false god. The false god is the small *"g"* god of money, the god referred to by the name *Mammon*.

Mammon is a devil of your money. He holds on to your finances.[5]

The Focus of Our Service

Jesus said it is God's desire that you serve Him only; He also said that you cannot serve two masters at the same time. When you focus on serving someone, you essentially place yourself face to face with that person. You fix your eyes on them. You position yourself in such a way as to be able to see them and hear them, so you can be prepared to carry out what they might request of you.

In the context of Matthew 6:24, it means to be in a position where you are facing your God in the presence of another god, a rival god. For example, if I am face to face and serving and being loyal to God and if I'm looking directly at Him, I cannot even see anyone else, because God fills my view. In order for me to see someone else, I must, to one degree or another, shift my attention, my focus, my gaze.

So while I am focusing on God, Mammon is speaking in my ear. This devil is speaking so much junk and murmuring so many temptations that, although I can't physically see him, I am aware of what he's offering me. Before I know it, I can begin to slowly shift my eyes away from God until my vision becomes divided. The devil uses what he offers me to catch my attention away from what I am looking at, which is God. You can see why God says that you cannot look in two places at the same time. You cannot be loyal to *the* God and *a* god all at once.

For example, it is physically and anatomically impossible for me to keep my eyes on my wife and also see a woman standing behind me. In order to see the person behind me, one of two things has to happen: either they have to move or I have to move.

However, the moment I move, I am no longer fully attentive to my wife. Because my eyes are not on her only, I have chosen to divide my focus and my attention (my "loyalty"), giving some of it to my wife and some to the other woman.

God says that it is impossible to split your loyalty. You can't take care of two competing objects at the same time. You can't take care of your wife and your secret girlfriend at the same time.

Tying It Together

All through Jesus' Sermon on the Mount (which starts with the beatitudes in Matthew 5), what seems to be a series of disjointed declarations as Jesus teaches on one subject and then another, is actually a focused sermon leading to a central point He wants to get across to the people.

Here is Jesus' teaching sequence following the beatitudes: In Matthew 6:5 He talked about how to pray. Jesus' concluded the topic of prayer with instruction on forgiveness (see Matt. 6:14-15). In Matthew 6:16-18, He talked about fasting. In verses 22 and 23, He talked about the lamp of the body, and in verse 24, He explained that you cannot serve God and Mammon.

As Jesus' teaching continued, however, He threw a seeming curve ball: Using the word *therefore*, He transitioned from the topic of God and Mammon (which began and ended in Matthew 6:24) to the next topic and verse. In Matthew 6:25, Jesus said, *"Therefore I say to you, do not worry...."*

In reality, by connecting verses 24 and 25 in this way, the two chapters (Matthew 5 and 6) become clearly linked. No longer do we read a series of disconnected statements. Instead, He connects them with this wrap-up sentence: *"Therefore...do not worry...."*

What do we worry about? Things. Stuff. The thing that was keeping the people from totally serving Christ Messiah as their one and only Master was their worry about *things*. Jesus went on to identify the things that worry us: *"what you will eat or what you will drink. . .your body. . .what you will put on"* (Matt. 6:25).

Then, after repeating the words *"do not worry"* (Matt. 6:31) Jesus added *"But seek first the kingdom of God and His righteousness, and all these things shall be added to you"* (Matt. 6:33).

God will take care of you! It's not necessary to serve two masters. . .you can't serve two masters. . .*you shall not* serve two masters!

The devil told Jesus, "Bow down to me just one time. Bow real quick and get up real quick—*pow!*—done! I won't tell anybody. And I'll give You all the kingdoms of the world" (see Luke 4:7).

Most Christian people would never, ever, serve the devil, yet some do. Most would simply not bow down to satan or to his cohort Mammon. Most would never even entertain the idea of following the ways of any member of the fallen angelic horde. Most Christians just wouldn't do it. . .*knowingly*.

Mammon Called Out

Here is what we have learned so far in our search to learn about and to expose the marching orders of the mysterious demon named *Mammon*:

1. God is looking for worshipers who will worship Him in spirit and in truth.

2. The devil wants to be worshiped too—in place of God.

The enemy wants us to bow down before him and grovel and kneel at his feet. He tempts us to do so, just as he tempted Jesus. But Jesus said to satan, *"You shall worship the Lord your God, and Him only you shall serve"* (Luke 4:8).

Jesus also told us, "Now understand, you cannot serve two masters" (see Matt. 6:24). This is not a choice between one Master being the true God and the other being just a "thing." This is between choosing the true God or choosing a false god by the name of *Mammon*. Jesus gave this example because Mammon is the entity that pulls people away from the true God.

Mammon is the demonic force that influences the way we handle money. Mammon is not money itself. *Mammon is the influence of the ungodly demonic that triggers how you relate to money.* Demons are fallen angels. Angels, by definition, are "messengers"[6] who are on assignment. Fallen angels, which simply means that they are fallen messengers. They now have different assignments than when they served God (before Lucifer was cast out of Heaven and they chose to go with him).

Now we know that there is at least one demonic spirit whose assignment is money. It is that demonic spirit (not the money itself, but the spirit in charge of it) who desires us to worship and serve him. To that, Jesus says, "You can't have it both ways; you can't worship and serve Me *and* Mammon."

But who would knowingly worship the devil? Who would knowingly bow down and worship the ungodly? Who would do it? You would never bow, worship, commit to, receive, acknowledge, or follow the devil as the lord of your life. You would never do it! At least not *knowingly*.

A Fatal Deception

Let's go back to chapter 4 of the Book of John. The same woman, the same well, and the same Jesus. We learned that God is looking for worshipers who will worship Him in spirit and in truth.

The woman at the well says in John 4:20, *"Our fathers worshiped on this mountain, but you Jews claim that the place where we must worship is in Jerusalem"* (NIV).

Jesus responds, *"Believe Me, woman, a time is coming when you will worship the Father neither on this mountain nor in Jerusalem"* (John 4:21 NIV). In other words, it's not about *where* we worship, it's about *who* we worship. He continues to explain: *"You Samaritans worship what you do not know; we worship what we do know, for salvation is from the Jews"* (John 4:22 NIV).

In effect, Jesus is telling her, "You Samaritans are worshiping all right, but you don't really understand what you are worshiping. In fact, you are sincere in your worship. The problem is not your sincerity; the problem is your ignorance. You are worshiping something you do not understand. You do not understand the system and the spirit realm that is behind what you worship."

Jesus' point is profound and intriguing. This is God in the flesh talking to this woman—the God who *made her!* He was saying that people actively worship, focus on, and serve something they think they know about, yet they have no clue what they are pouring their time and attention into.

The woman was a Samaritan. While accepting the Pentateuch (the first five books of the law: Genesis through Deuteronomy), the Samaritans tended to deny the validity of the Psalms, the books of the prophets, and the historical books, Samuel, Kings, and Chronicles. Because the revelation of the coming Messiah was proclaimed through the prophets, the Samaritans had a limited and incomplete revelation of Him. They were worshiping incompletely. Therefore, the woman did not know or understand what she was waiting for. Still, she said, *"I know that Messiah (called Christ) is coming"* (John 4:25 NIV). Basically, she said, "Yes, we Samaritans are aware of that. We know about this worship thing. We know that Messiah is coming."

To that, Jesus responded simply and directly: "I am that one" (see John 4:26). He told her, in effect, "You were in danger of missing Messiah because you were worshiping the wrong thing, which is distracting you from worshiping the true God. But I, Messiah, am now here and I am telling you whom to worship and how to worship. So you have an opportunity to get on the right track."

Few of us deliberately worship the devil. But the contrast Jesus made was not between God and the devil, it was between God and Mammon—the demon whose assignment is money, "things," "stuff." His assignment is prosperity and material blessings, including what you eat, what you drink, what you wear, the necessities of life. It is this demon who wants us worried about those things, distracted by them, focused on them, freaking out about them.

Mammon's goal is to nudge us toward full panic mode and make us feel like that's a normal reaction. He whispers in our ears, "You don't know if you'll be able to make ends meet," he whispers in our ear. "How are you even going to pay your bills this month? You don't make enough money. You need a raise. You need a new job. Look over there—that family makes more money than yours does!"

We worry, worry, worry. And yet, we love Jesus.

Jesus says to you, "What you're looking for is right beside you." He told the woman, *"I who speak to you am He"* (John 4:26).

The devil is so shrewd. One of the reasons many Christians do not recognize him is because he does not wear flaming red underwear, carries no pitchfork, has no horns on his head, and doesn't have a long, pointy tail. People assume that if they haven't seen someone running around with a pitchfork and red long johns, they haven't seen the devil.

The devil is too smart to be obvious. He wears designer suits. He drives Beemers and Benzes. He wears $400 sunglasses and $800 shoes. Because the challenge that we have in life is all about *things*.

Worry, WORRY, W-O-R-R-Y!

Most people would never say that they have worshiped the devil or even fallen prey to his ways. But have you ever worried about overdue bills? Have you *ever* been worried about money?

It is said that the top two causes of relational breakups are money and sex. The problem with the woman at the well was sex. She had been married five times and had finally given up and chose to shack up.

Many things can distract us from worshiping God. So how should we handle that which competes with Him? How do we get delivered from worrying about things? How do we change our mind-sets and attitudes about God and the subject of money? What happens in settings where we're enthusiastic and excited and involved when talking about the deeper things of life with our loved ones, yet, when the subject of money comes up, our attitudes change?

I've noticed this pattern in my own life. I'm fine until someone says something about money. That's when my whole countenance changes. Why does that happen? In a marriage, it seems like you can talk about almost anything, but talk about money and the climate changes.

What can we do? How can we handle this better? It is damaging our worship to God. How do we rise above that negative attitude and get a grip? How do we rise above mediocrity and soar on the wings of God?

A good first step would be to ask God to *ban from yourself and from your home a selfish spirit.* Don't read this as a criticism; *read it as a revelation about the tactics of the enemy.* This is not a chastisement of your ways; it is a challenge to learn new truths and respond in new ways—God's ways.

Whom Do You Worship?

To find out who it is you are truly worshiping in your life, ask yourself two questions:

"Looking back over the pattern of my life, whom have I *really* chosen to worship?"

Next, ask yourself, "Am I *sure* about that?"

Somebody is after you. He wants your worship. His name is Mammon, and he is diabolically clever. Many of us are already worshiping him, and we don't even know it. If, for the sake of getting riches, you bow down to the devil just once, then you have the riches—and you have a master over you other than God. It can only be one or the other. Whom do you worship?

Endnotes

1. *Biblesoft's New Exhaustive Strong's Numbers and Concordance with Expanded Greek-Hebrew Dictionary.* CD-ROM. Biblesoft, Inc. and International Bible Translators, Inc. s.v. "proskuneo," (NT 4352).

2. Does satan really have possession or control over everything, as he suggested when he tried to offer it all to Jesus? Or is satan a deceiver and the father of all lies, as John 8:44 says? Hebrews 2:8 clears up this issue, stating that God

put all things in subjection to Jesus: *"He put all in subjection under Him, He left nothing that is not put under Him."* In other words, the devil tried to offer to Jesus what already belonged to Him—just like a con man who tries to sell a person their own watch. Jesus' response to the devil's deal was for the devil to get lost, *"for it is written, 'You shall worship the Lord your God, and Him only you shall serve'"* (see Luke 4:8). There are many other con jobs the devil and his cohorts (including Mammon) try to pull on us every day.

3.   *Biblesoft's New Exhaustive Strong's Numbers and Concordance with Expanded Greek-Hebrew Dictionary,* s.v. "mamonas," (NT 3126).

4.   *Webster's Dictionary of the English Language Unabridged,* Publishers International Press, New York, 1977.

5.   *Winston Dictionary,* John C. Winston Company, Philadelphia, 1954.

6.   *Biblesoft's New Exhaustive Strong's Numbers and Concordance with Expanded Greek-Hebrew Dictionary,* s.v. "mal'ak," (OT 4397) and s.v. ángelos (NT 32).

Notes

Chapter Two

FOR THE LOVE OF MONEY

. . . Thither, winged with speed,
A numerous brigade hastened; as when bands
Of pioneers, with spade and pickaxe armed,
Forerun the royal camp, to trench a field,
Or cast a rampart. Mammon led them on—
Mammon, the least erected spirit that fell
From heaven; for even in heaven his looks and thoughts
Were always downward bent, admiring more
The riches of heaven's pavement, trodden gold,
Than aught divine or holy else enjoyed
In vision beatific. By him first
Men also, and by his suggestion taught,
Ransacked the centre, and with impious hands
Rifled the bowels of their mother Earth
For treasures better hid. . . .
—John Milton; from *Paradise Lost, Book I*

W HEN Jesus said in Matthew 6:24, *"No man can serve two masters: for either he will hate the one, and love the other; or else he will hold to the one, and despise the other. Ye cannot serve God and mammon"* (KJV), it wasn't because it is illegal or tough to serve two masters. He said it because it is actually *impossible* to serve two masters.

In his epic poem *Paradise Lost*, John Milton gave an artistic depiction of hell. In his details of the dominion of the damned, Milton pictured satan as a fallen commander-in-chief. He depicted satan, at various points in the poem, as being surrounded by his various generals. Names were given such as Molech and Dagon and Osiris and Belial. All of those names but one (Osiris) come directly out of Scripture.

There is an interesting scene conjured by Milton in this *Paradise Lost* poetic classic, in which satan is seen standing with another god at his side. This satanic and demonic god is identified by Milton as *Mammon* (the same one who followed satan in the rebellion against God and against Heaven). As we see in the passage, Milton's Mammon is in the posture of looking downward, continually gazing at Heaven's streets of gold, but never into the eyes of the Lord.

As Milton's poem goes, Mammon fell along with the hordes of satan into the place called hell. He also became the god who discovered precious metals at the core of the earth. Milton portrays this Mammon as the one who is obsessed with the wealth available in earth's core.

Obviously, the poem is myth. But this Mammon depicted in Milton's *Paradise Lost* is the same Mammon identified by Jesus in Matthew 6. This same Mammon, when found in several old cultural languages such as Aramaic and Syriac, has a name that is related to wealth or riches or money.

In Matthew 6:24, Jesus identified the name *Mammon* as belonging to a spirit being. He revealed this Mammon as an alternative object of human worship; but He clarified and declared that it is impossible for those who truly worship God to also worship Mammon. Jesus essentially said, "You cannot serve God and this Mammon being."

In the Nigerian language there is a "god of the waters" whom they call *Mammion of the Waters* (related, obviously, to Mammon). In the Nigerian culture, this god of the waters, rivers, and seas has such an impact that he affects and alters the minds, attitudes, and behavior of human beings. Mammion alters normal behavior, turning it into abnormal behavior.

Again, this is an obvious connection, if only etymologically, to the god of whom Jesus spoke, the god called Mammon, the spirit being who operates specifically in relationship to finances, money, material blessings, and possessions. That's his domain. His mission is to influence our attitudes with regard to those things. The question is: Has the demon Mammon been doing a job on you?

Jesus gave two options of service for us: We can serve God or we can serve Mammon, but we cannot serve both. The choice is ours.

A Devil's Deal

We learned earlier, in John 4, that God is Spirit and that He must be worshiped in spirit and truth. God is seeking, examining, investigating, searching for those who will do as He says: Worship Him in spirit and in truth. God is not looking for church members. He's not looking for choir members. He's not looking for preachers. But he is on a search mission for worshipers. God wants your worship. He wants your worship in spirit and in truth. Those are the kind of worshipers He's looking for. He's not looking for those who would "worship" Him outside of spirit or outside of truth.

God is also looking for those who will serve Him. But remember, He says you cannot serve both Him and Mammon, because either you will love one and hate the other, or you would be loyal to the one and not the other (see Matt. 6:24). So, God wants your worship, He wants your service, He wants your love, and He wants your loyalty. Satan wants the same things from you. He even tried to tempt Jesus into giving him all of those things in exchange for all of the riches of the world. "Just bow down one time," he tried to entice Jesus, "and it's all Yours" (see Luke 4:7).

Jesus tells us, "Sure, you can give your worship, love, service, and loyalty to satan if you like—but you can't then give it to the Father too." Jesus' proposition raises an interesting question: If Mammon is in fact an alternative to God (an anti-God); if Mammon is part of a demonic hierarchy against God, a demonic horde of principalities and powers arrayed against God (as described in Ephesians 1:21 and Ephesians 6:12); and if I can't worship God and Mammon both, *why would I want to?* Why would I try to serve God and then serve satan?

Think about it. If the enemy approached you and asked you to worship him and serve him, you would probably say no. Most people would. This begs another question: Who would knowingly worship Mammon? Who would worship him while fully realizing that's what they're doing? A more important question is this: *Is it possible to worship something and not really know who or what it is?*

The answer may surprise you.

Let's return to John 4:22-23 and the woman at the well. In verse 22, Jesus told the woman, *"You worship what you do not know....But the hour is coming...."* Jesus said that the hour is coming, changing from something that *is* to something that *will be.* He was just about to say that true worshipers will worship the Father in spirit and truth. Notice, He didn't tell the woman that she wasn't worshiping and should start doing so. Instead, He acknowledged that this woman worshiped. But He told her, essentially, "You don't fully understand or comprehend what or who it is you are worshiping."

Right there, Jesus indicated that *it is possible to worship and not know what it is we are worshiping.* Mammon, Jesus said, is indeed an alternative to—but not an addition to—God, because it is spiritually impossible to worship both. Yet, some of us, thinking we are doing the one, do not realize that we are actually doing the other.

My former professor, Dr. David Hocking, taught me that, as believers, we have three enemies:

1. *THE WORLD:* It wants to give you success—*without God.* However, Jesus asked the rhetorical question: *"What does it profit you if you gain the whole world and lose your soul?"* (see Mark 8:36).

2. *THE FLESH:* It wants to give you pleasure—*without God.* Romans 13:14 warns us, however, to *"...make no provision for the flesh, to fulfill its lusts."*

3. *THE DEVIL:* He wants to make you religious—*without God.* Here's what Second Timothy 3:5 says about people who have a form of godliness, but deny its power: *"Have nothing to do with them"* (NIV).

The devil will do anything to keep you away from the truth, knowing that you can only truly worship God in spirit and in truth. It's not an issue of whether you worship, it's an issue of whom you worship, how you worship, in what realm and dimension you worship, and by what power you worship.

The devil's deal to Jesus was, "I'll give you all of this if You will bow down and worship me." But Jesus knew exactly what satan's deal meant: "Once You bow down, Jesus, You will have turned away from God who sent You, and You will have made me Your god."

Satan wants you to be religious. There is a religious spirit in the world today. The growth and spread of so-called New Age religions, humanistic philosophies, New Age gatherings, and a focus on materialistic and secular ideologies, are nothing more than distractions to make you feel spiritual and religious and deep—as you march on your way to hell.

"I am the way, the truth, and the life," Jesus said in John 14:6, *"No one comes to the Father except through Me."* I know that sounds dogmatic—maybe even *bulldog*-matic—but it's what Jesus said.

You cannot serve God and Mammon. Period. If you are, then you're living the devil's deal.

Mammon's Influence Over Money

Mammon, the ungodly spirit-being, attaches itself to the four areas of finances, money, material blessings, and possessions. If we can worship Mammon and not know we're worshiping him, then we need to learn what we can do to prevent that from happening.

Mammon influences us in many ways. The two biggest areas of his influence over us are *power* and *provisions*. Let's examine each of them.

Power

We have learned that it is possible to be influenced and not even be aware of it. The devil influences us—often without our even realizing it. The Bible says that the devil is a deceiver, a liar, and the father of lies (see John 8:44). Mammon is a demonic spirit who is very *subtle*. He will distort your concept of power. In fact, it is the influence and mind-set of Mammon that makes us create and quote such colloquialisms as "the almighty dollar," because the connection of the dollar to the word *almighty* empowers money beyond the will of God—who alone is Almighty.

It is as though there were some kind of inherent power in money itself that causes us to think that the more money we have, the more *something* we are. We believe that our worth is related to the power we have based on how big our paychecks or bank balances are.

We ascribe a basic, inherent power to money. To the degree that we do this, we are under the influence of Mammon. It is this ungodly demonic force that assigns to money and materialism a power that those things actually do not have. There is no inherent power in money; money is inanimate and amoral. But there's a power *behind* money. And by now, you know his name.

You can determine what spirit power controls your money, because your money is empowered at the point (and to the degree) that you surrender either to the inanimate object itself or to the power behind it. In other words, *we surrender power to that which we serve.* We will serve that which we trust. When we trust in the power of "stuff," then we are already under the influence of Mammon, because we are ascribing power to material things.

The phrase *the almighty dollar* is, by definition, a misnomer. There is no power in money. We talk about money; we sing about it; we desire it. Sometimes we get upset when people talk about it. In fact, a very popular song was written about money in 1973; it depicts the attitude and the power that we ascribe to money:

> *...Money money money money, money*
> *Some people got to have it*
> *Some people really need it*

...Y'all do things, do things, do bad things with it

You wanna do things, do things, good things with it

...Cash money—dollar bills, y'all

People will steal from their mother

For the love of money

People will rob their own brother

...People can't even walk the street

Because they never know who in the world

they're going to beat

For that lean, mean, mean green

Almighty dollar, money

For the love of money

People will lie, Lord, they will cheat

...People don't care who they hurt or beat

...A woman will sell her precious body

For a small piece of paper it carries a lot of weight

Call it lean, mean, mean green

Almighty dollar

...Money is the root of all evil

Do funny things to some people

Give me a nickel, brother. Can you spare a dime

Money can drive some people out of their minds....

—The O'Jays, *"For the Love of Money"* Epic/Legacy Records, January 1973

Our culture has attributed to money a power that is not of God. Money is not almighty. God is almighty. Mammon distorts our concept of power by ascribing to stuff and to money and to the things that come with them an inherent power that we crave and desire and will do anything for— steal from our own mothers, rob our own brothers, to get what money can buy.

Provision

Mammon is very subtle because it raises the issue and the question of what or whom is our source. What or whom is your provider? What or whom will have your needs met?

Because of the materialistic process that drives our culture, money, for many of us, has become our goal and, in essence therefore, our provider. We assume that all we need will come if we only have enough money. The source of our happiness then becomes, simply, more stuff and more money.

As a result, we commit our lives to getting more of it and to being in greater relationship with it, because we assume that money—or whoever puts money in our hands—is our source. For many of us, our source is a job, because it is through our jobs that we get our money. Some people have investments and count on them to bring in what they need. When this attitude operates in Christians, we inadvertently reduce God to a kind of prized exotic animal in a petting zoo we visit now and then. He becomes someone we "visit" in between our efforts to get our needs met through and by money. And who is lurking behind that money and our quest for it? The ever-present Mammon.

This quest takes many different forms. Some people rely on others or on relationships to be their source. In some cases, single folks seek their source in the form of a mate who will provide for their needs. That attitude suggests that their minds and their lives are already being influenced by the god, Mammon. When you assume that your needs are met by money, then money becomes your provider, your source, your goal. And if that thinking is in you, Mammon has done his job well.

If you are a wife, for example, and you assume that your source is your husband, then you are actually veering into sin. When you are looking for someone other than God to be your source and to provide for you, it is sin. When your answers for the direction of your life are based on how much money you have or you wish you had or you are trying to get, your mind is already under the influence of the god, Mammon.

This presents an interesting conflict for believers: If your love is for "money money money money," as the song says, then you love Mammon! And it is that spirit behind money who is actually drawing you to that money in the first place.

Remember, however, that Jesus already warned that we can't love both God and Mammon. If we are trying to do both, a tension exists. It is a fundamental conflict that divides the heart. If we are obsessed with money and with things; if money has become the answer to all of our needs, then God is not the one whom we are loving. He is not our source—money is.

If money is your source, then money is what you will serve, because you will always serve your source. You are loyal to your source. You hold to and worship your source. This is why God says you cannot serve or worship both Him and money—particularly.

Work: Temporary Assignments From God

If you go to work each week, ask yourself *why* you go. Why do you get up early, all the while wishing you could sleep in? Why do you bother getting ready for work, just to endanger yourself with all of the crazy drivers out on the crowded streets?

Why? Why do you work? What are you expecting from your job? Is it just money? Your answer is important because, if you work for the money, then you have placed yourself under the influence of Mammon.

We need to understand that our jobs are among the many temporary assignments we receive during our days in this earth realm. Your job, your career, is what God called you to do. It's what He has gifted you to do; it's your assignment. It is where God has planted you for this season of your life.

If God is first, then your job and your boss are only channels through which your source (God) will meet your needs. The assignment may last 10 weeks, 10 years, or 40 years, before God moves you on to your next assignment on earth (or promotes you to Heaven). Those assignments are not your source; they are not in charge of providing for you. Only God is. And rest assured that He will move you in and out of assignments during your earthly lifetime. He will do it as He sees fit, in accordance with His plan. Also rest assured that He will make certain you are provided for along the way.

If I love God with all my heart, my mind, my soul, and my spirit, then He is my source. I look to Him to meet my every need. No matter what job I do, no matter who my boss is, he or she is merely the conduit, or channel, through which God has chosen to meet my needs. At any point in my life, I can trust that my source has decided to meet my needs through whichever job He has me in. Once I get my head straight about that, I'm not worried about the economy or about what's hot and what's not. I'm not flustered about the world economic situation or about financial crises.

Once I understand who my provider is, I'm not looking for the boss, the union, or the corporation to be my source; I know that my source is my God. And if God chooses to meet my needs through the job I'm in, I will praise Him for it. Likewise, if He chooses to meet my needs someplace else, I'll still give Him praise, because the job is not my source. My God is my source.

If you are between jobs right now, don't worry, God is just "channel surfing" for you: He's got control of the remote and He's about to—*click!*—change the channel through which He will bless you.

Don't worry; it is always His good pleasure to provide for you. You are standing right now because God is in control of the remote. He's about to click onto the new channel that will provide for your needs.

If your current assignment is ending and you're about to lose your job, the new one is about to begin. He's still your source. He can change channels in a nanosecond. That's why you have to be careful how you act when you're on a job. That's also why employers have to be careful how they treat you on that job: you're not just somebody sitting in a cubicle; you're a representative of the King of the universe, and you're showing them how Jesus can work. If they mess with you too much, God will—*click!*—change channels.

That is not to say that God always sends us where we will be appreciated, as the story of Joseph attests. Sometimes the channel you're on is challenging. Joseph was mistreated, abandoned, and under-appreciated—for years! Yet, there came a day when Pharaoh elevated Joseph to the second-highest position in all of Egypt.

There are times when the channel you are on is pleasant. In fact, for some people, the channel they are on at this moment has them feeling pretty good about themselves, or even puffed up in pride. If pride is involved, God might change the channel again, and put them someplace where they can learn that He and only He is worthy to get all the glory.

Our sole source is God the Creator. If you are between jobs, still trusting Him, believing in Him, and having faith in Him, then simply know, trust, and believe that He is about to click on the new channel through which He will supply all of your needs!

Our attitude should be *Surf, Jesus, surf! Keep on clicking, God, to the right place where I can give You all the glory, all the time.*

A Subtle Perversion

Power and provision are just two of the areas that Mammon usurps in relation to human beings. Mammon is a skilled pervert. He is skilled at perverting the relationship between God and His people.

We are to serve and love the Lord with all our heart, mind, soul, and strength (see Deut. 6:5), demonstrating that He is our Master and we are His servants. If you believe that now, or if that is where you want to be, then make this declaration:

> God is my Master. I am His servant. That is God's order. God is Master; I am servant. All that I have is at His disposal because I am His servant. All that I have is but an instrument through which I worship and serve Him, because God is my Master and I am His servant.

What the subtle spirit of Mammon has managed to do is to infiltrate and encourage a contemporary theology that perverts the order of God. Instead of

God being our Master and our serving Him, money becomes our master and we look to God to serve *us*.

In other words, I come to God because He is the one who gives me my stuff. I come to Him not for His name's sake or for who He is; instead, I treat Him, in very subtle ways, as though He were here mainly to provide for my needs. Instead of seeing God as my Master, I act as though He were my favorite slave, a person whose function it is to get me stuff.

The one who should be my Master, I make my servant. The subtle desire, the unintentional prayer is, "God, help me, please. Give me, please. More please." How often do you hear people praying prayers that consist only of praising Him for who He is and for nothing more? No asking for stuff, no petitioning for anything. Just praise.

Truth be told, most of us go to church and ring our holy bell and wait for God to snap to and ask us how He can serve us. Why is this? Because theological extremists have focused the Gospel and our relationship with God almost completely on issues related to what we get, what we want, what we have gotten, or what we have not gotten from God.

That is a material-based relationship; not a relationship based purely on love. Our very first response to God, the reaction that should leap from within us in His presence, should be as it was with Abraham in Genesis 22, Jacob in Genesis 31, Joseph in Genesis 37, Moses in Exodus 3, Samuel in First Samuel 3, and Ananias in Acts 9: *"Here I am,"* not "Here's my hand." We are His servants.

Instead, the Church is well down the road to becoming as materialistic, humanistic, and secularist as the world outside. The relationship between Master and servant has reversed. We stand before Him wanting more things—and we whine and moan and complain when He doesn't give them to us, or when He doesn't do it quickly enough for us.

The enemy is a subtle pervert! It is a perversion that only looks to God for what we can get from Him. That's not how we worship Him in spirit and truth; that's worship according to what we need or want. This so-called worship has been orchestrated by Mammon. Much of the Church is serving this god and doesn't even know it.

God wants to bless you and—yes!—God wants to meet your needs. Yet, God is not looking for you to perform for Him in order to get stuff from Him. Nor is He expecting perfection from you before He provides for you; He is looking for you to worship Him first, last, and always—because of *whom He is*. He wants you to seek His face, not just His hand.

Biblical truth has been distorted by the devil and his minions, and we are buying into it. Mammon has taken our relationship with our Maker to unspiritual extremes and perverted the very relationship between God as Master and us as His servants, to the point where money and wealth have become our real god, and the true God is simply the middleman between us and more "stuff."

As a pastor and leader of a flock that God has blessed me to guide and shepherd, I repent for every time I may have said or implied anything that has made people think that they come to God just to get stuff from Him. I repent if I have ever made one Christian think that when they give their offering, or when they give their money, or when they tithe, they're getting the favor of God or are getting in good standing with God. I repent if I ever made anyone think that God would deliver them more possessions or improved finances or a better job or a bigger house or more money based on their giving. I repent if I have ever insinuated or taught or said anything like that. I repent. That is a perversion of the true worship of God. That attitude is not the heart of a servant. It is a cunning perversion of the devil.

Too many Christians go to a place of worship and are put on a guilt trip because they're not in the $100 line or the $50 line or the $20 line. That is not God! God never speaks to us out of guilt. He never speaks to us to condemn us for what we don't have. He speaks to us wanting us to be grateful for whatever we do have.

With the very slick manipulation of the god of Mammon, we have taken truth and bastardized it and prostituted it. We have divorced it from the very nature and character of God. The spirit of Mammon has so permeated the Church that we look for ministry gimmicks to hustle people into giving more money—and nobody seems to want to shout, "This is not of God!"

This perversion of truth is not the Spirit of God; it is not the will of God; it is not God's way. We ought to worship God for who He is. We ought to thank God for who He is. We ought to praise God because there but for His grace we would get exactly what we deserve. Each of us ought to praise and worship God—even if He never gives us another dime. He is worthy to be praised not because of what He's done, but because of who He is—and nothing more. He would be worthy even if He hadn't done what He just did for you.

Jesus was right when He explained to the Samaritan woman at Jacob's well that you could bow down and serve and not even know what or whom you're worshiping. We buy into the stuff and the junk and the things that are on television and radio and on crusades and conventions and meetings, all of which have exactly two things to do with God: little and nothing.

The people of God are struggling with guilt and with persecution and weakness of faith because they are telling themselves, "I keep doing this and it's not working." The reason it's not working is because your spirit has been distorted by the god Mammon. Bind that spirit today! We've been bamboozled! Hoodwinked! Fooled! We have mishandled the blessings of God because of a distorted concept of God's blessings.

Many people across America are one paycheck away from disaster and ruin, because everything God gives to them, they eat up. We must begin being better stewards of God's blessings. You cannot serve god and Mammon.

Notes

Chapter Three

A HEART PROBLEM

LET'S take a look at a classic example of how Mammon can influence us:

> *But there was a certain man called Simon, who previously practiced sorcery in the city and astonished the people of Samaria, claiming that he was someone great* (Acts 8:9).

This verse introduces a fellow named Simon, who worked in witchcraft, or sorcery. By identifying himself as a man who practiced witchcraft, he positioned himself as somebody "great." If you have to tell people that you are great, odds are you aren't all that great.

I used to go to conventions where pastors and ministers and preachers could buy just about anything they wanted. One place sold a robe that even glowed in the dark. It was iridescent and had a cape attached to the back of it. Printed on the cape were the words *The Pastor.*

Let me tell you something: if you have to wear a sign that says you're the pastor, then you probably aren't pastoring much of anything. If you have to keep telling people you're the head of the house, you probably aren't the head.

Simon, the sorcerer, told people he was someone great. The passage in Acts 8 goes on to say that Simon was someone *"to whom they all gave heed, from the least to the greatest, saying, 'This man is the great power of God'"* (Acts 8:10). Simon was working witchcraft. He had people convinced that he was of the very power of God.

Another version says, *"all the people, both high and low, gave him their attention and exclaimed, 'This man is the divine power known as the Great Power'"* (NIV).

The introduction of Simon continues:

> *And they heeded him because he had astonished them with his sorceries for a long time. But when they believed Philip as he preached the things concerning the kingdom of God and the name of Jesus Christ, both men and women were baptized. Then Simon himself also believed; and when he was baptized he continued with Philip, and was amazed, seeing the miracles and signs which were done* (Acts 8:11-13).

Here's the picture: Simon was a guy who lived in the world of witchcraft; he was a man clearly away from the Lord. But he received the Word of God, was baptized, believed the Gospel, and his soul was saved—the whole nine yards. He had been a worker of witchcraft, but he got saved. He was one who had made a great living in witchcraft. He had a great reputation for working sorcery, but he became a believer.

The story continues:

> *Now when the apostles who were at Jerusalem heard that Samaria had received the word of God, they sent Peter and John to them, who, when they had come down, prayed for them that they might receive the Holy Spirit. For as yet He had fallen upon none of them. They had only been baptized in the name of the Lord Jesus. Then they laid hands on them, and they received the Holy Spirit. And when Simon saw that through the laying on of the apostles' hands the Holy Spirit was given, he offered them money, saying, "Give me this power also, that anyone on whom I lay hands may receive the Holy Spirit"* (Acts 8:14-19).

This is a man who had worked voodoo, sorcery, and witchcraft, amazing all of the people. Then he came to know Christ and he turned his life around. When Peter and John came to town, they blessed and laid hands on people and the people received the Holy Spirit. Whatever they did was something that Simon *saw*, something that was *observable*.

Whatever that was, Simon looked at it and said, "Well, lookee here! How'd you guys do that?" He then reached into his pocket and said, "Look man. Lemme talk to you over here. I used to do stuff back in the day myself, you know. Maybe you can help a brotha out here. How much would you charge me for some lessons on how to do the things you're doing? Whatever power that is, I want it."

No doubt Simon, in the past, had traded inside secrets with other sorcerers and purveyors of magic. Back in the day, he was probably accustomed to purchasing new voodoo gimmicks to amaze crowds, make a few dollars, and make himself famous. He thought the apostles had a new hustle going on. So he asked, "How much will you charge me, man, to show me how to do those tricks? How'd you do that? Whatever that power is, I'll pay for it."

> *But Peter said to him, "Your money perish with you, because you thought that the gift of God could be purchased with money! You have neither part nor portion in this matter, for your heart is not right in the sight of God. Repent therefore of this your wickedness, and pray God if perhaps the thought of your heart may be forgiven you. For I see that you are* [two things:] *poisoned by bitterness and bound by iniquity"* (Acts 8:20-23).

Peter said to Simon, "Your heart is not right, because you thought you could buy what God gives freely." It's a *heart problem*. We know that Simon's heart was messed up because Peter told him, "You have been poisoned by bitterness and bound by iniquity." So, two things were wrong: Simon was poisoned and he was a prisoner. Why? Because he came to the Kingdom with the world's mind-set.

Understand that the economies of the world operate on the principle of *buying and selling*, while the Kingdom of God operates on the principle of *giving and receiving*. Peter told Simon bluntly, "There's something wrong with your heart, because you're trying to operate in the Kingdom under the principles of the world."

Simon knew that if you want to get something through the buying and selling system, you have to cut a deal. What he didn't realize is that the Kingdom of God doesn't operate that way. The Kingdom system is based on giving and receiving. Simon had a heart problem because he was poisoned by bitterness and was a prisoner of iniquity (see Acts 8:23). He was a saved man who still thought and operated in the ways and principles of the world.

Iniquity

Let's look at iniquity first. *Iniquity* is a word that is related to, but is slightly different from the word *sin*. The two are often interchanged, but etymologically speaking, there's a nuance, a slightly different spin, to each word.

Sin is an *act;* we commit sins. Sin is related to what we *do.* Iniquity is more technically the *attitude* behind the action. Iniquity is what's in our hearts before it comes out through the body in the form of actions. Iniquity has to do with the mind-set—that which is inside of us and prompts us to do things that are not in line with God's ways. So, while what we do in these cases is called *sin,* it did not start there. It started with whatever it was in the mind and heart that made it seem OK to do what we did.

If sin is iniquity on display, then iniquity paves the road to sin. *Iniquity* means to be bent toward something, to be twisted, to be distorted. "You are bound with iniquity" involves more than what you just did; it indicates that there is something in your heart that made you *want* to do what you did.

What's in your heart is iniquity. You are bound up as a prisoner of your "bents." You are bound over to the "twists" and distortions of your mind. What you have done must be repented of, because your heart is messed up. It's off kilter. It has become that way because there's poison in your heart: the pollution of your heart trapped you in the distortions of your mind.

Here's the problem with iniquity:

> You shall have no other gods before Me.... you shall not bow down to them nor serve them. For I, the Lord your God, am a jealous God [thou shalt not cheat on Me] *visiting the iniquity of the fathers upon the children to the third and fourth generations...* (Exodus 20:3,5).

God says that when we bow down to serve other gods, the effect of our bowing is not limited to our own lives. Because iniquity is the thing inside us that caused us to bow—and here is perhaps the most frightening thing about iniquity—*it is transgenerational.* This means that the iniquity in us can show up through our children, our children's children, and their children, all the way to the third and fourth generation.

The emphasis in the passage is on iniquity. God does not say that sin is passed down; He says that the iniquity is passed down—the bent, the twist, the proclivity; the tendency is what passes down through the generations.

This means that there is something in us that allows our iniquities to show up to the third and fourth generation of our offspring. God says that when I turn from Him and bow down to other gods, there is a trans-generational consequence to my idolatry. So, if I do something in my life, what I did is not necessarily passed on to my children (though they can certainly suffer the effects of it). However, the tendency to do what I did is passed on to my children's children and *their* children.

For every sin you commit in your life, you must ask yourself how it will impact your grandchildren and great-grandchildren. The iniquity and attitude that caused you to sin could cause a domino effect and endanger your future generations.

The traits of the parents become the tendencies of the offspring. What you see in me, you may very well see in my grandchildren. Peter the apostle said that Simon the sorcerer was a prisoner to his tendencies. According to Exodus 20:5, Simon's heart condition could have been visited upon his offspring to the third and fourth generations.

How does this relate to money and Mammon? The following passage makes a connection between Mammon, iniquity, and true riches:

> *He who is faithful in what is least is faithful also in much; and he who is unjust in what is least is unjust also in much. Therefore if you have not been faithful in the unrighteous mammon, who will commit to your trust the true riches?*
> (Luke 16:10-11)

In this passage, Jesus explained that the question of whether we will be entrusted with true riches is related to how we handle "unrighteous mammon."[1] Mammon knows that if he can move my tendency to sin into an actual committing of sin, then he has prevented me from being trusted by God as a steward of His true riches. Worse than that, he may have also prevented my future generations from being trusted with true riches, because of the trans-generational effects of my iniquities to the third and fourth generations. He will have killed many blessings with one stone.

True Riches

"True riches" are determined by our attitudes toward material blessings. God blesses us with true riches based on how we handle material things such as possessions, money, etc. The implication is that the "true riches" spoken of in Luke 16:11 must go beyond my money, my house, my car, my possessions. Jesus said I am trusted with true riches (spiritual riches) from God based on how I handle the material things.

Simon's problem was that he thought there was power in money. He thought his money gave him enough power to buy more power. It was a classic influence of the god Mammon, who is the empowering personality behind "stuff."

Simon basically said to Peter and John, "I've got enough money (power) to buy the trick you just did." Remember, the mind-set of the world revolves around buying and selling. "Sell the secret to me, Peter," Simon said. "I've got enough money to buy it."

Simon didn't realize that the *true riches* come based on our handling of material blessings and *material blessings* are but a channel and vehicle through which the Kingdom of God is expanded.

To Bless Others *Through* You

One of the goals of Mammon is to pervert the understanding that God works through people and that He blesses others through us. That principle of blessing requires relationship among all of the parties. Therefore, the devil wants to sabotage relationships—between God and man, between Master and servant.

Mammon knows that everything we have is to be used by God's servants to serve and glorify Him; but if Mammon can get us to see stuff and materialism and the things of this world as our goals, we will hoard everything instead. If this god can train us to reach for and desire things instead of reaching for and desiring God, he will have successfully undermined the critical relationships that yield blessing. Then, when I come to God, it will only be to get more things.

God does not bless us with the things of this world just so that we might have things in this world. The purposes of His blessing are threefold:

1. To enhance the Kingdom of God.

2. To further the name of the one who gives us the blessings.

3. To bless others through us.

Deuteronomy 8:18 tells us that God is the one who gives us the power to gain wealth—to get a job, to pay our bills, to provide for our families and loved ones. But He does not give us jobs or income merely so we can get more possessions. He gives us material wealth to affirm His covenant, which is to bless us and bless the world through us.

In other words, He's trying to get a blessing to you in order to get a blessing *through you.* It works like this:

- I can't bless you until I've received a blessing. *But…*

- God won't bless me if He knows I won't bless you. *However…*

- If God knows He can get a blessing through me to you, *then…*

- He'll get the blessing to me, knowing that I will get the blessing to you. *Thereby...*

- Blessing both of us. *Furthermore...*

- If you then bless someone else with your blessing, *then...*

- The original blessing God bestowed on me will have echoed into the lives of *many.*

The spirit of Mammon distorts this simple yet powerful paradigm. Even the Church has unwittingly found herself in the position of becoming a sort of prostitute, hawking her God to get more stuff from the world. That is a spirit of Mammon, and many in the Church are bowing down to it. It thwarts the purpose of God's blessings. You are never the end purpose of a blessing to you. God wants to get a blessing to you *only so He can get a blessing through you.* Once you receive a blessing, the best thing you can do is to become aware of somebody who has a need. Then, as soon as you are blessed, you can pass a blessing on to them.

What many people want to do is receive their blessing and immediately run off and enjoy their blessing. It's an attitude of *I got mine—good luck getting yours.*

The Strongman Binds

It is crucial to understand how subtle this devil, Mammon, is. How has he been able to trick intelligent, sophisticated, savvy Christians—not to mention the entire world? In Matthew 12:24, the Pharisees claimed that Jesus was casting out demons by the power of Beelzebub, the devil, the ruler of the demons. In His response to them, Jesus again connected iniquity (unrighteousness) with Mammon:

But Jesus knew their thoughts, and said to them: "Every kingdom divided against itself is brought to desolation, and every city or house divided against itself will not stand. If Satan casts out Satan, he is divided against himself. How then will his kingdom stand? And if I cast out demons by Beelzebub, by whom do your sons cast them out? Therefore they shall be your judges. But if I cast out demons by the Spirit of God, surely the kingdom of God has come upon you. Or how can one enter a strong man's house and plunder his goods, unless he first binds the strong man? And then he will plunder his house" (Matthew 12:25-29).

In this passage, Jesus explained that the enemy, the strongman, the devil, can come into a house, bind or tie up the owner of that house, and then become the strongman who controls that house. In order to take control of a house you must first come in and bind or take control of the strongman; then you can take the house back. Therefore, if you are going to retake a house that the enemy has taken over, you must first *bind the strongman.*

The Greek root for "house" is *oikos,* a word that has two connotations: it is literally a building or a house and it also implies a family or a household[2] such as the house of David, the house of Isaac, the house of Abraham. It doesn't only mean the place where the person lives; it is referring to his family. What Jesus said is that the enemy has the ability to attack your family, your *house,* and take control of it. In order to take control back from the strongman, *he must be bound.*

How do you bind Mammon?

Jesus laid out the scenario as it occurs in the spiritual realm and affects us in the physical realm:

> *When an unclean spirit goes out of a man, he goes through dry places, seeking rest, and finds none. Then he says, "I will return to my house from which I came." And when he comes, he finds it empty, swept, and put in order.* [Notice that the unclean spirit says he will return to "my" house—he calls it *his* house!] *Then he goes and takes with him seven other spirits more wicked than himself, and they enter and dwell there; and the last state of that man is worse than the first. So shall it also be with this wicked generation* (Matthew 12:43-45).

We have seen that the enemy can attack your house, meaning your family. We also know that he can be bound and cast out. However, just because he's out doesn't mean it's time to shout! The Bible says that when he's cast out, he goes on the prowl. He searches for a place to rest, a place to reside, a place to regroup, a place to which he can attach himself. If he can't find one, he says, "I'll go back to *my* old house and bring some of my buddies with me—my seven brothers. You thought it was bad before; wait until I return!" In the end you're worse off than you were in the beginning.

Our Weaknesses: A Bitter Pill

Simon the sorcerer's problem was that he was prisoner of his iniquities, a captive in his own house of iniquities. Mammon is a demon who looks for your weaknesses. Simon's bitterness was his weakness. We don't know why he was bitter; Scripture doesn't tell us. But something must have happened to Simon at some point in his life that made him bitter, angry, and insecure.

We know this because Simon spent his life telling people how great he was. His bitterness became the "hook" to which Mammon could attach himself. That's what Mammon does; he looks for our iniquities. And when he pounces on our weaknesses, he distorts the way we handle life.

Peter tells Simon, in effect, "You've got a heart problem, Simon. There's bitterness in your heart and the enemy has found rest on it."

The King James Version of Acts 8:23 uses the phrase "gall of bitterness." The Greek word for bitterness in is *pikria*. This is acrid wickedness; an extreme and offensive wickedness that can lead to harming others. It is a bitterness that acts out in anger. The word implies a bitterness that manifests in envy and resentment of others.[3]

Have you ever met someone who never seems to be having a good time, or who never expresses joy? Something...somewhere...sometime...somebody poisoned them. And that poison spread throughout their spiritual being. The toxin becomes a weakness and a target for the enemy. It determines and influences our attitudes toward life and governs how we deal with things, how we handle blessings, how we handle success, how we relate to others. *Mammon is a venom that exploits our tendencies and our iniquities.*

That's one of the reasons why so many people have trouble in relationships. They know something is wrong, but they can't seem to figure out what it is. In those situations, it's important to keep in mind that it's not always about you. That person had a problem before you came into his life. Somebody broke his heart, somebody messed with her, somebody did her wrong, somebody flattened his spirit. You're just getting the fallout of it. What happened to people frames the way they look at life—and how they look at you. They're insensitive, cold, cruel, and hard. It's not about you.

The problem is not just what we do, it's the attitude in the heart that becomes a target for the enemy. It influences our entire perspective on life so that we can't even get blessed or handle it properly when we do. Life becomes a hustle, a game we run on people, including friends and family members. We try to buy them, influence them, control them. All because somewhere inside there's a bent, a twist, that the enemy has staked a claim on and he's now claiming as *his* "house" (see Luke 11:24 and Matt. 12:44).

A Heavenly Antidote

Simon had a problem, not just with his sin, but with his iniquity—not just with his actions (his transgressions), but with his attitude (his iniquities). It wasn't just what he did, but what was in his mind causing him to do it. Well, I've got good news for you: Isaiah 53:5 says that Jesus *"was **wounded** for our transgressions, He was **bruised** for our iniquities. . . ."*

Let's take those two phrases one word at a time: a *transgression* is an act. You transgress when you cross the line or go over the boundary. It's something you do—it's external. Jesus was wounded for what you do. A wound is also external. If you are shot, cut, or sliced, you can see the wound. The Bible says that He was wounded (externally) for what I do (externally). However, He was bruised, not for my transgressions (what I did), but for my iniquity (the thing inside that caused me to do what I did).

A while ago, when my wife and I were on vacation, she walked past a table and accidentally bumped her thigh. She didn't even think about it.

Later that evening she said to me, "Honey, look here at my thigh."

"What's wrong?" I asked.

"Look at this bruise," she answered in amazement, pointing to a large discoloration on her thigh.

There was no blood. She wasn't cut. But the bruising indicated that there was internal damage; there was bleeding under her skin.

You can cover up a bruise; you can hide it under a three-piece suit, a beautiful dress, or artfully applied makeup. Yet, what you can't see is often what hurts even more than what you can see.

What you can't see on the outside is what sticks with me long after I put a bandage on my hurt. What you cannot see is what keeps me up at night. What you can't see is what has affected or brought about my attitude. It's what makes me angry or bitter or sad. It's what makes a person ungrateful or judgmental. It's what makes a child treat others the wrong way. There's *something happening underneath that others cannot see.*

He was *bruised* for what's underneath the "skin" of my life, what's *behind* my actions and attitudes. My iniquities. He was bruised for what I *am.* My tendencies. My weaknesses. However, He was *wounded* for what I *do*—for my actions and deeds, which are precipitated by my tendencies.

Yet, if we confess our sins, He is faithful and just to *forgive us* of our *sins*, our doing evil; and to *cleanse us* from our *iniquity*, our unrighteousness (see I John 1:9). He cleans out the wound. He stops the damage.

Simon wanted to use money to buy the power of the Holy Spirit. He had a heart problem, and it was revealed by his attitude and tendency and words and actions in his encounter with the apostles. That heart problem gives us a glimpse of Mammon at work. It reveals that his influence in the world can affect and infect many areas of our lives.

What's the solution? *The first step is prayer.* "Lord, I give You my heart. Clean up my heart. Clean up my bitterness. Clean up my disappointment, my pain, my insecurities. I give You my heart. I give You my soul."

Maybe you say, "Now why did I talk to my wife that way when we were discussing my paycheck?" Sure, Mammon was doing his work on you, but there was also something underneath the skin that made you talk to your spouse that way. There was something distorted that only God can straighten out. You want to be more loving, you want to be more sensitive, you want to be more patient, more caring; but every time you try, something rises up in you that is still bent. You were hurt and Mammon will take advantage of it every time the topic comes up.

Or maybe you're a woman enamored with men who have great monetary means, and you're drawn to them even if they compromise their walk with God around you—thus compromising your walk with God. Maybe that was your mother's attitude toward men and money. In speaking of a habit or trait in someone, my mother would often say that they "came by it honest," which meant they acquired that trait from one of their parents. Rest assured, Mammon will be right there, encouraging you on in that generational bent.

If you see something in your life that you cannot handle all by yourself (even if has nothing to do with finances, money, material blessings, and possessions, which are the areas of Mammon's specialty), you need to immediately take it to the Lord. Allow Him to handle it for you, to dig out and clean out the wound, and heal you. God works through people, using those gifted in counseling as instruments of revelation and deliverance in the lives of people struggling with iniquity issues. You may look at things you have done in utter disbelief that you could have done them. In fact, you probably can't believe anybody would do those things.

You don't know why you do things like that, but you know you can't handle it all by yourself. That's why you can turn on someone in the twinkling of an eye, and with your tone of voice, your attitude and mannerisms, absolutely destroy them. And yet you say you love them. That's a heart problem. That's a bent, an iniquity, a tendency. But I've got news for you: He was bruised for your iniquities.

God is Spirit. They that worship Him must worship Him in spirit and truth. The truth is to pray like this: "I want to worship You, God, but I have some things in me that need Your healing touch. There are things in me that only You can put a stop to. I don't want to pass them on. I don't want to contaminate anyone, infect anybody, hurt anybody, set bad examples for my children and grandchildren, or cause them to suffer for my iniquities."

The first step in removing the grip of Mammon over your life is to take your heart problem to the Lord. He wants to heal you. He wants us fully spiritually fit to deflect the blows that the devil and his cohorts continually throw at us throughout our lives here on earth. God wants us to be able to withstand them and be delivered from the power of Mammon.

Endnotes

1. *Strong's Dictionary.* The Greek word for *unrighteous* is "adikos" (G94), which has the same meaning as the Hebrew word "avah" (H5753), which is the root of the word "avon" (H5771), which is the Hebrew word for *iniquity* used in Exodus 20:5.

2. *Biblesoft's New Exhaustive Strong's Numbers and Concordance with Expanded Greek-Hebrew Dictionary.* CD-ROM. Biblesoft, Inc. and International Bible Translators, Inc. s.v. "oikos," (NT 3624).

3. *Strong's Dictionary,* "pikros" (G4089), acrid, bitter.

Notes

Chapter Four

DELIVERANCE FROM MAMMON

Mammon is like fire: the usefulest of all servants, if the frightfulest of all masters!
—Thomas Carlyle, *Past and Present*

I T is woven into the very character and nature of God that He is a blesser. We have learned that the assignment of the fallen angel named Mammon is to attach himself to the areas of finances, money, material blessings and possessions, and to distort and pervert our attitudes and actions toward the blessings of God. The result is that we unintentionally end up serving and honoring the demonic spirit Mammon. It is just as Jesus said in John 4:22: it is possible to serve and worship a god without knowing whom or what it is you're worshiping.

We have discovered that few people would willingly or knowingly bow down to the enemy and to demonic and devilish forces; yet we have learned that it is possible for us to be caught up in his wretched web because of the attitudes that we have toward the material and financial blessings that God pours into our lives.

Solomon, the writer of Proverbs, offers a powerful prayer in response to the lies of Mammon:

> *Two things I request of You (deprive me not before I die):* **remove falsehood**
> **and lies far from me**; *give me neither poverty nor riches—feed me with the*

food allotted to me; lest I be full and deny You, and say, "Who is the Lord?" or
lest I be poor and steal, and profane the name of my God (Proverbs 30:7-9).

Let's begin with the first part of Solomon's prayer: *"Remove falsehood and lies far*
from me." In other words, "Steer me away from lies. Do not let me be influenced
and impacted by those who speak negativity into my life, or declare my demise, or
say that I have no worth. Shield me, protect me from the mind-set that perceives
no value in my life." He is asking God, in essence, "Remove me from liars. Protect
me from people who, by their very nature, lie. Spare me from those who, through
their lies, feed into my own sense of insignificance."

He is praying that God will help him see himself as God sees him, to avoid
people who would devalue the man God created him to be, and to be separated
from lying tongues and negative influences that would try to foster a sense of
nothingness within his heart. He also asks God for help in affirming both the gifts
God had given him and the greatness God has purposed for him to attain.

The apostle Paul said, in First Corinthians 15:33, *"Bad company corrupts good*
character" (NIV). Some people will never become all they can be in God until they
start hanging out with a new crowd. You will never attain the heights God wants
for you and you will never be who God wants you to be as long as you hang around
people whose minds can't reach into the next minute, let alone the next day or the
larger future, where God is trying to take you. Don't hang around those who cannot see in you what God sees in you.

Balance and Attitude

Now let's look at the second part of Solomon's powerful prayer, his plea for
humility in the context of a God who provides and blesses:

. . .give me neither poverty nor riches—feed me with the food allotted to me;
lest I be full and deny You, and say, "Who is the Lord?" or lest I be poor and
steal, and profane the name of my God (Proverbs 30:8-9).

Solomon says, "Don't give me poverty and don't give me riches." There's no *name it and claim it* and no health, wealth, and prosperity message in that verse. Extreme Word of Faith prosperity is not there.

"God, if You give me riches," Solomon is saying, "I'll probably handle it the wrong way and even deny that You gave them to me. I'll lie. I'll defame Your name. I'll embarrass You, my God. I'll bring shame to Your Kingdom. But, don't give me poverty either, because then I'm going to cheat, I'm going to steal, I'm going to get desperate, I'm going to lie, I'm going to do whatever I will, and I'm going to shame Your name that way, too. Just feed me my portion, my daily bread."

This is not a prayer against being blessed. That's not what this prayer is. This is not a vow of poverty. It is a verse that says, "Lord, I do not want anything that does not come from You, but I want everything that You have allotted as my portion. I am not asking for riches. I am not asking for poverty. I am saying that I want everything that You want me to have." The essential truth in this part of Solomon's prayer is: "Lord, I'm relying totally on You."

That's a tough prayer for many people to pray. You might be wishing you had never seen that proverb. Many people simply rush on past it. *"Feed me with the food allotted to me."* When we truly acknowledge God as our source, we are satisfied in knowing that we will have as much or as little as He says is our portion.

God's provision is that simple. It only gets complicated when the love of money drives us out of God's will. He knows what we need and He provides for those needs through the channels He selects. He blesses us with that which He says is our portion. Through preparation, prayer, providence, and other people, God navigates and orders the steps of your life to put you into those channels of blessings that He has reserved for you. Mammon hates this message of truth and will do anything to prevent you from believing it.

Solomon recognizes that he is speaking to *the* God who has the power to provide, the power to bless, the power to meet needs. That is why Solomon said, *"Give me neither poverty nor riches."*

What a powerful prayer to pray! He says, "Father, You are the God who provides. So I ask, first of all, that you give me neither poverty nor riches. *Let me not go to either extreme.* Don't let me be poor, because if I'm poor, I know myself—I'll get it one way or the other, even by stealing. And I know that if I steal, I will shame Your name."

What is poverty? How poor do you have to be to be poor? You have to be careful who you ask that question, because some of us are so poor we don't even know we're poor. According to the U.S. Census Bureau, if you are single and you make less than $10,991 per year, you're poor. If you are a family of three raising one child and you make less than $17,330, you are poor.[1]

In truth, *poor* is a relative term. What would it take to get you to say that you are poor? The question could be asked this way: "What would it take for me to say 'I'm not poor?'" There are countries where people live on less than one dollar per day. I visited the Democratic Republic of the Congo a few years ago and found out that those serving in the army there earn just $10 per month–that's 33 cents a day!

The Bible describes two types of lack: *poverty* and *abject poverty*. "Poor" has to do with those who lack the *conveniences* of life. "Abject poverty" are those who lack the *necessities* of life. For example, Acts 3:10 talks about the man who begged at the temple gate. He was in abject poverty; he was a beggar and lacked the necessities of life. By contrast, Mark 12:42 and Luke 21:2 talk about a poor widow who gave two pennies at the temple. The text suggests that she had the necessities of life, but not the conveniences. Yet, both people were considered poor.

I want to suggest to you that poverty is a mind-set. Poverty is not about a dollar sign. *Poverty is an attitude.*

Mind-sets of Wealth and Poverty

"Give me not poverty," Solomon prayed in Proverbs 30:8-9. This passage, I suggest, has nothing to do with a dollar sign. Instead, it involves a mind-set toward material, financial, and monetary blessings. It points to an attitude of poverty—a spirit of poverty—that has nothing to do with where you live or what kind of clothes you wear.

For example, some people were able to go to college because somebody sacrificed. Maybe your grandmother or mother cleaned people's bathrooms to make a way for you to attend college, to pay the bills, to keep food on your table and clothes on your back. She may have been monetarily poor, but there was something about her generation that carried a sense of pride and dignity about them in spite of what was in their bank account—or what was not. There was an ability back in their days to handle a dollar wisely.

On Thursday, October 29, 2009, my 93-year-old mother went home to be with the Lord. She was a unique example of humility and pride. She and my dad taught us children that if we get something into our head, no one can ever take it from us. They instilled a particular mind-set into us—one based on faith in God, plus a solid work ethic.

My momma used to stretch a dollar. She knew how to stretch the food in a pot, too. She could take cold turkey or chicken and it would be around for weeks. We were still eating cold turkey when Christmas rolled around. For us, the biggest thing about Christmas was that it brought a change of diet.

Momma used to go shopping, not so much for clothes, but for fabric. She had a file full of dress patterns. She had an ability to "make do" on meager income—with dignity.

Poverty is not a dollar sign; it's a mind-set. There is an attitude that is contrary to poverty, even in the context of earning little income. *"Give me neither poverty nor riches,"* Solomon said (Prov. 30:8). How much wealth do you need to have to be wealthy?

According to Deuteronomy 8:18, God is the one who gives you the power (the ability) to get wealth. In today's terminology, we would state that as, *God gives us the ability to earn a paycheck.* But Deuteronomy says that He enables us "to get wealth." Most of us don't categorize what we get paid as wealth. But wealth, just like poverty, *is a mind-set.*

Bill Gates was worth $40 billion in 2009. He had a rough year. His fortune was down $18 billion over 2008—and he was still the wealthiest American.[2] How much money does it take to be wealthy? If someone were to say to you, "When you get that job, you're going to be wealthy," how much would you have to be making to agree with them? How much money per year is "wealthy money" to you?

When Senator John McCain was asked by Pastor Rick Warren during the 2008 presidential election cycle, "How much money does it take for a person to be considered rich," Senator McCain responded, "Five million dollars." Many people would say that if you earn one million dollars annually, you're rich. But if Bob Johnson, the founder of BET (Black Entertainment Television), made a million dollars in one year, he would be on the verge of bankruptcy. If Oprah Winfrey made a million dollars in a year, the news media would report that Oprah's going under.

Would you feel good if you were making $100,000 per year? Would you smile a little more when you read in Deuteronomy 8:18 that God is the one who gives you the power to get wealth? Would your six-figure income cause you to read that verse differently? Many people would smile and say, "Oh yes! I'm making $100,000!" Let me tell you something: *wealth is a mind-set.* A million dollars is bankruptcy for some people, and $100,000 is rich for others.

Wealth is not so much about your bank account; it's about your attitude *despite the size of your bank account.* There's a mind-set spirit of poverty, and there's a mind-set spirit of wealth.

A key to deliverance from the influence of Mammon is having an assurance of *who you are.* If you see yourself as a royal priesthood and a child of the King, your whole attitude changes, because you recognize your source. And you realize that it's not your boss. Your source is not your job. Your source is not being in the union. Your source is not the economy. It's not your 401(k). It's not the stock market.

Always keep in mind that your job is simply the channel through which God has chosen to bless you. In the struggle to keep free from the effects of Mammon, it is crucial to realize that *God alone is your source* and that your boss is merely the one whom God has put in the line of succession in determining how much blessing He will get to you. And, since God, your source, never sleeps or slumbers (see Ps. 121:4), you can sleep at night!

As Solomon wisely stated, *"A good name is to be chosen rather than great riches, loving favor rather than silver and gold"* (Prov. 22:1).

Two Lesser Demons: Poverty and Pride

Mammon is in charge of two lesser demons that attack us in the areas of finances and material blessings, tainting our responses to the blessing of God. They are the demon (or spirit) of poverty and the demon (or spirit) of pride.

Poverty

If my economic standing is, by somebody's estimation, low or lower than others, then I become a candidate for, not so much monetary poverty, but a *mind-set* or *spirit of poverty.*

Pride

If, on the other hand, God blesses me by someone's standard of wealth, I become a candidate for an attitude or *spirit of pride.*

Both of these are based on *the levels of blessings that God pours into my life.* If I conclude or sense that I am being paid "less than" I think I deserve, then I fall victim to, or become a candidate for, a spirit of poverty. It has nothing to do with the size of my paycheck or bank account. It is the spirit of poverty that causes me to compare my earnings (or what I *think* I should be earning) to what somebody else is earning.

My struggle is that there's a mentality that the god of mammon releases whenever I recognize and then quantify the provision of God in my life—either the abundance of the provision or the lack thereof. If I think God has not given me enough, then I am operating in the spirit of poverty. If, by contrast, I think that God has given me a great deal, I could fall prey to the spirit of pride.

Take the example of someone buying a beautiful new home. A buyer with a spirit of poverty would explain the purchase this way: "Well, you know, it was in foreclosure, so I didn't pay that much for it. It's a nice little house, but I would never have paid what it was really worth. I wouldn't have spent that kind of money."

The spirit of poverty focuses on the blessing as though it is undeserved. This spirit has to justify and explain and even apologize for living in a house that big. This spirit causes the buyer to worry: *When the girls see me in this house, they're probably gonna think I'm all that and a bag of chips.*

By contrast, the buyer operating in a spirit of pride would think: *I am all that and a bag of chips!* This spirit focuses on self. It says, "I really wanted to buy an even bigger house. Still, you ought to see the house I bought. It is some kind of house. And, you know, if I hadn't hooked up with the seller, I wouldn't have gotten the deal that I did. They knew nobody could have this house but me. Actually, it's worth even more than I paid for it. I had the money to pay more, but they closed the bid too quick. It was a steal. Either way, you know I wasn't going to let this house get away."

The issue here is about extremes. *Don't let me go to either extreme,* as Solomon asked God in Proverbs 30:8.

The spirit of poverty comes over us when we become so concerned about what other folks will say about our blessings that we minimize and downplay God's gifts to us. *A spirit of poverty will make you ashamed of your blessings* to the point where you find yourself apologizing and rationalizing and quantifying the bless-ings God bestows on you. Your fear of the opinions of others prevents you from having a testimony about the great hand of God in your life.

Part of the problem is the people we hang out with. If you spend time around people who worry about how you got your blessings, then you're hanging out with the wrong crowd. You need people around you who will rejoice with you every time they see a blessing in your life. You need people who will celebrate with you when you celebrate. You don't have to explain how you got it; you don't have to explain why you got it, you just have to know that it was nothing but the grace of God.

The spirit of pride wants to puff things up and make the blessing seem like more than it is. Take a prideful woman with a nice purse, for example. When you admire her handbag, she replies, "Oh, this thing? I've had it forever—it's an original, you know. Very expensive. Had to get it on backorder 'cause they were in such high demand." The truth is, she bought it down some back alley where a man was selling knockoff name-brand purses out of his trunk.

The spirit of pride always wants situations to look better and bigger than they are. The prideful person enjoys blessings, but they'll only tell you where their stuff came from if they think you'll be impressed by it. They'll tell you if they got it at Nordstrom, but they won't tell if they got it at the little private boutique down on the other side of the tracks that sells fakes—Heaven forbid anybody should know where they really buy their "stuff"!

In summary, *the spirit of pride wants to take the credit for the blessing.* It claims to be the source of the blessing, as though it came because the person was so smart, clever, and sharp. Instead of giving the glory to God, the prideful individual will take the glory themselves: "I knew that person and he cut me a deal." "I know this person, and she got me in." "I make a high income, so I qualified for it." It's all about *I, I, I.*

By contrast, *the spirit of poverty wants to downplay the blessing.* It apologizes for it. "Well I didn't really want to." "Well I shouldn't have." "Well I normally would never." "I don't really deserve it anyway." They're all, *No, No, No.*

The spirits of pride and poverty are alike in one fundamental way: they take the focus off God and center all the attention on *me, me, me!*

An Attitude of Gratitude

What is the place of healthy balance in our response to the blessings of God, where we don't react with pride nor with poverty?

What God wants from us is an *attitude of gratitude.* The child of God who truly loves the Lord says, "It was nothing but the grace and mercy of God." This person has a spirit of thankfulness that gives all the glory to Him.

What keeps us balanced is when we get the blessing and we give the credit to the Blesser. You stay in balance when you recognize that you didn't deserve the blessing in the first place.

The balanced attitude thinks, *Had it not been for the Lord on my side, where would I be?* God looks for this spirit of gratitude. If you handle a "little" with gratitude, then you're in line for a big blessing. *It's how you handle what you have that prepares you for what you're going to get.* If God can get you into an attitude of gratitude, then He can get great blessings into your life.

A story is told about a billionaire who was giving a lecture at Howard University. He was asked by a student how he had gained his wealth, and he began to explain how he had done it.

The student asked him, "What part do you believe God played in your wealth? What is your relationship with God?"

The wealthy man answered, "God had nothing to do with this. It was all me. God wasn't the one who went into the board meetings and planning meetings. I was." That is the spirit of pride at work. Proverbs 16:18 says, *"Pride goes before destruction, a haughty spirit before a fall."* A year after that student asked the rich man that question, he had lost half of his net worth (and that was before the financial earthquake of 2008). He had failed to acknowledge or even realize that it was God who had given him the idea that brought him the billions of dollars of income, who had given him the mind to get the degree and to learn the skills that made him rich.

How would you respond if you were asked to recount the blessings of your life and how they came about?

God is looking for a grateful heart. Walk through your memory and acknowledge how good God has been to you. Walk through your house and think about how good God is. Thumb through your checkbook and see how He has paid your bills with a zero checking account, yet you never had a check bounce. Take stock and count the ways God has blessed you. Go through your medicine cabinet at the symbols of God's provision when you didn't even have the money to pay for the medicine you needed. See how good God has been. Look at your children and remember all the times that God has kept them safe, leading them around dangers seen and unseen.

It was not because of your education. It was not because of the letters behind your name. It was not because of who your relatives are. It was not because of the connections you have. It was nobody but God on your side. We need to have a spirit of thanksgiving that says, *"My God has supplied all of my needs according to His riches in glory"* (see Phil. 4:19). Look back over your life and see how faithful God has been. Say, "Thank You, Lord!" Don't be ashamed to give God the credit and the glory.

Don't apologize for where you live—thank God for where you live! Don't apologize for the car you drive—thank God for the car you drive! Don't let the devil fool you. Don't even let him try to make you apologize for the blessings you have received from God. Do not be ashamed of what He does for you. Be grateful that you wake up in the morning in a warm bed. Be thankful for being healthy. Appreciate having food on the table. He does it because He loves us. He does it so we will pass it on to those in need.

Always bear in mind Solomon's prayer: "Give me only my daily bread. Otherwise, I may have too much and disown You and say, 'Who is the Lord?' Or, if I become poor I might steal, and so dishonor the name of my God" (see Proverbs 30:8-9).

Build a foundation on the concrete, solid-rock blessings of God, and not on the sandy, stubbly, self-centered deceptions of the devil, Mammon.

> *Man is a mere phantom as he goes to and fro: he bustles about, but only in vain; he heaps up wealth, not knowing who will get it* (Psalm 39:6 NIV).

Endnotes

1. "Poverty Thresholds for 2008 by Size of Family and Number of Related Children Under 18 Years," U.S. Census Bureau, http://www.census.gov/hhes/www/poverty/threshld/thresh08.html (accessed November 21, 2009).

2. www.Forbes.com/2009/03/11/worlds-richest-people-billionaires_land.html.

Notes

Chapter Five

THE WAR OVER WORSHIP

As we investigate the workings and mission of the god named *Mammon*, it is crucial to keep in mind one of the basic things that "protects" us, that keeps us pure and unpolluted from his influence: God is not looking for "religionists," He's looking for *true worshipers* who will worship Him His way—in spirit and in truth.

So far we have learned the following:

- God desires our worship.

- Those who worship Him must do so in spirit and in truth.

- God desires our service and wants us to live our lives for Him.

- God wants us to serve Him out of love ("love the one, despise the other").

- God wants us to serve Him out of loyalty.

- We cannot serve two masters (it's either God or Mammon).

The admonition of Jesus in Matthew 6:24 and Luke 16:13 that you *cannot* serve God and Mammon, does not say we *should not* do it or that it would be a tough thing to do, but, as the verses emphatically state, you *cannot* do it. It is a spiritual impossibility to serve two masters simultaneously.

When Jesus says that you cannot serve God and Mammon, He is implying that serving Mammon is an option. As we have learned, the grammatical phrase-ology of Matthew 6:24 treats the word *mammon* as referring to an actual *being*. In other words, Mammon is a spirit being *capable of being worshiped*. This indicates that the two "masters" have something in common: each of them can be served. They are not unfeeling, or unperceiving; they are sentient, aware beings. It is not an incongruent comparison between worshiping God and worshiping a thing. Rather, Mammon is actually a demonic force, a part of the hierarchy of hell, a member of the hordes that follow satan (formerly known as the archangel *Lucifer*).

Thus, the principalities of Ephesians 1 and Ephesians 6 are fallen angels (demonic messengers on assignment) who follow satan and comprise his army—the legions of the demonic. As we have learned, the assignment of the particular fallen messenger Jesus refers to as Mammon is to influence our attitudes toward money, riches, finances, and material possessions. His mission is to influence how we handle, in general, all our possessions in life and, more specifically, money.

A Battle for Your Mind

Alexis de Tocqueville wrote:

> The love of wealth is therefore to be traced, either as a principal or an accessory motive, at the bottom of all that the Americans do: this gives to all their passions a sort of family likeness. . .[1]

In seeking to influence our attitudes toward money and material blessings, the lie that Mammon speaks into our lives, the distortion of reality that he suggests, is that money has power. Power to give you something. Power to bring you something. Power to make you something.

It is Mammon's goal, his mission, his assignment, to *empower money* and in so doing, to imply (and to train and convince us) that money is our source—of happiness, of fulfillment, of significance. Any idea or concept or teaching or philosophy anywhere in the world that is similar to this one is the result of the influence that Mammon has managed to exert upon human minds over the eons.

It's a battle for your mind. It's a battle designed to drive you to see money as the source of your significance in life and in the world. This is, of course, a massive deception, because our actual source is God—and God alone (whether or not we acknowledge that). It is God only who gives us the power, the ability, the where-withal, to gain wealth.

True worship acknowledges God as our source. What Mammon wants to do is to distort our relationship with God in any way possible. His specific mandate is to do that through our relationship to finances, money, material blessings, and possessions.

Yet, if God is our source and we are to worship Him, then He is our Master and *all that we have is at His disposal.* If Mammon cannot budge the Christian from this truth, then Mammon will try to pollute, twist, and reverse that relationship by telling us something like, "Okay, sure, God might be involved as the conduit through which you humans get money and 'stuff,' but it only works if you connect the 'God dots' exactly as He commands and if you color inside His lines perfectly, and push all the right God buttons."

Over the centuries, many Christians have been subtly steered by this Machia-vellian pro referred to by Jesus as Mammon (who has been around a *lot* longer than we have) to subliminally view God as some sort of cosmic genie who will grant us our wishes if we don't misstep; or that if we manipulate Him just right, we're in the money.

The flaws with this thinking are twofold:

1. No human on earth can reach that level of "doing life perfectly" and in full accordance with God's laws. Only Christ did that (see Rom. 3:23).

2. It's not about *doing*; it's about faith (see Eph. 2:8-9). Faith (like worship) *starts in the heart.* Unconditional faith in God as our only source is one of the things that protects us from the machinations of Mammon. (And Mammon doesn't only focus on tricking Christians; he has been very resourceful in his work

on nonbelievers, too, training the world to see God as only one of many possible sources.)

This Mammon mind-set, this "monetization" of Christianity, has crept even into the Church. It hovers and subconsciously permeates the activities of increasing numbers of churches throughout Western cultures today. Many Christians do not give to or bless others purely in honor of the God who is their source and who gave them the power to earn an income. Instead, in a very subtle way, they "spin" the truth and give in order to get something in return. This is not an act of worshiping our provider, nor does it acknowledge His provision.

Worship and Provision

When Jesus talks about God looking for worshipers, and then He makes the statement, "you cannot serve God and mammon," He is raising the issues of *what or whom is at the center of your worship, and what or whom is your source.*

Since Paul said, *"My God shall provide all your needs"* (see Phil. 4:19) and we know that He gives us the ability to gain wealth (see Deut. 8:18), then how does God do all of this? How and where do worship and provision come together? What is the relationship between my worship of God, and His provision for me?

One of the ways to understand a concept in Scripture is to exercise a fundamental hermeneutical principle called *the law of first mention.* This means that if you want to understand a law, concept, or word, you must try to ascertain where it was first utilized. This will give you an idea of what that law, concept, or word means when it is used later in Scripture.

So, if Apostle John writes that God is looking for worshipers who will worship Him in spirit and in truth, then we need to look at where the word *worship* first appears in the Bible:

> Abraham said to his young men, "Stay here with the donkey; the lad and I will go yonder and worship, and we will come back to you" (Genesis 22:5).

This verse indicates that some things had taken place between Genesis 12 (when God told a childless Abram to leave his country and go to the new land he would be given) and Genesis 22 (after God had changed Abram's name to Abraham and blessed him and Sarah with a son named Isaac, whom God was now telling Abraham to sacrifice). After many events had occurred, Abraham was going to be tested on Mount Moriah. Between Genesis 12 and 22, God had promised Abraham three things:

1.   He would bless him.

2.   He would make him a nation.

3.   He would bless the nations through him.

God made these three promises to Abram in Genesis 12. Then, in Genesis 15, God reiterated that He was going to give Abram a son—indeed, that his offspring would be as numerous as the stars in the heavens. The problem was, Abram had no son—he had no offspring at all. If God was going to keep His promise, then He had to give Abraham a male child. But at the time God made His promise, Abram and his wife were well past the age of conceiving.

Yet, the impossible happened: well into their old age, God miraculously gave Abraham and Sarah a son, Isaac (see Gen. 21)—the very child God had promised. Isaac was the miracle baby through whom God would fulfill His promise.

Fast-forward the story to Genesis 22. God had promised that He would give Abraham innumerable offspring, which would require sons, plural. So, in Abraham's old age, God miraculously gives him a baby. It is not only the baby that Abraham had been looking for all his life, it is the very child God promised him many years earlier. This son, Isaac, whom Abraham and Sarah had in their old age, was the miracle baby through whom God was going to fulfill His promise.

After all of that back-story, now Genesis 22:1 makes sense: *"Now it came to pass after these things that God tested Abraham…."* Here comes the test of Abraham: *"Take now your son, your only son Isaac*[2]…*and go to the land of Moriah, and offer him there as a burnt offering on one of the mountains of which I shall tell you"* (Gen. 22:2).

The word translated "burnt" here is taken from the Hebrew word *olah*,[3] from which we get our English word *holocaust*. God is telling Abraham, in effect, "Take this boy that I gave you and make of him a holocaust."

A few years ago, my wife and I visited Auschwitz, Poland. We walked through the prison camp where hundreds of thousands of Jews were burned. During the Holocaust, the Nazis would first take the prisoners and put them in big rooms that looked like community showers. The people thought they were going to have a chance to get cleaned up; instead, the guards would lock the doors and pipe poison gas through the shower fixtures. Then they would take the bodies to conveyor belts that led into ovens. There the bodies would be burned.

What the Nazis did with the bodies of their victims was essentially what God was telling Abraham to do with his son Isaac: "Make of him a holocaust." Burn him. Abraham was to put the boy on an altar, strike the fire, and offer him as a burnt offering to God.

Genesis 22:1 says: *"After these things God tested Abraham."* Between Genesis 12 and Genesis 22, God had been teaching Abraham some things. Then, in Genesis 22, God tested him on the lessons. You could say that Abraham had been "going to church" from Genesis 12 to Genesis 22. Then suddenly, in Genesis 22, God pulled a major pop quiz on him.

I guarantee you this: if God has ever taught you anything, *He will test you on it.* It's the way He works. He will never test you on material that has never been taught; but *He will test you at some point on what He is teaching you right now.* It's a spiritual principle: what the teacher teaches, the teacher tests.

Whom Do You Trust to Provide?

Abraham had learned that God is a God who provides beyond that which is natural. He provides in the face of obstacles and impossibilities. He also learned that, without question, God is his absolute, sole source. "Let's see if you've learned that lesson, Abe," God was saying, in essence. "Take the boy I gave you into the land of Moriah and put him on the altar and slaughter him. Then burn him." If

God is truly your source, there will be a time in your life when you will reckon with that issue and you will be tested on it. God will come to you and say, "Let's see what you've learned."

There used to be a game show back in the 1950s called *Who Do You Trust?* (I know, I know—most of you reading this book are too young to remember the 1950s!) It was originally hosted by Johnny Carson. In the quiz portion, Carson would tell the male contestant the category of the upcoming question; the man would then have to decide whether to answer the question himself or "trust" the woman to do so. The show revolved around who you would trust to give you the right answer.

At some point in your life, you're going to have to deal with the same question: Who do you really trust? Is my destiny in the hand of the economy? Is my future in the hand of the stock market? Where does my destiny lie? In whom do I trust?

Here's what God told Abraham to do:

> *"Take now your son, your only son Isaac, whom you love, and go to the land of Moriah, and offer him there as a burnt offering...."* So Abraham rose early in the morning and saddled his donkey, and took two of his young men with him, and Isaac his son; and he split the wood for the burnt offering, and arose and went to the place of which God had told him (Genesis 22:2-3).

In verse two, God said, "Go." In verse three, Abraham went. His obedience was immediate. There is no space between verse two and verse three. Abraham obeyed instantly, without resistance or complaining or even questioning God. God was in the process of making Abraham a capable father, not just of Isaac, but of *nations.*

Many people wrestle with issues of obedience. It's not an issue of wondering what they should do in life, but an issue of obeying that which God has already clearly instructed them to do. Their problem is not that they are uncertain about what God has told them to do. It's whether they want to do what God says. *It's an issue of simply obeying Him.*

Continuing with the story from Genesis:

> *Abraham said to his young men, "Stay here with the donkey; the lad and I will*
> *go yonder and worship, and we will come back to you" (Genesis 22:5).*

See the word *worship* in this verse? This is the first time in Scripture where that word is used. Remember, Jesus had told the woman at the well that God is on a search mission. He's searching for those who will worship Him in spirit and in truth. He's searching for worshipers.

> *So Abraham took the wood of the burnt offering and laid it on Isaac his son;*
> *and he took the fire in his hand, and a knife, and the two of them went together.*
> *But Isaac spoke to Abraham his father and said, "My father!" And he said,*
> *"Here I am, my son." Then he said, "Look, the fire and the wood, but where is*
> *the lamb for a burnt offering?" And Abraham said, "My son, God will provide*
> *for Himself the lamb for a burnt offering." So the two of them went together*
> (Genesis 22:6-8).

When Isaac, the sacrificial lamb, carries on his own back and up to the mountain, the wood upon which he will be placed to be made a sacrifice,[4] theologically this is called a *type;* it foreshadows, most often, something fulfilled in Christ. In other words, here is a scene in the Old Testament that will be fulfilled centuries later in the life of Christ. Isaac becomes a picture, a foreshadowing, of Jesus, who carried the wood (the cross) upon which He would die on top of a hill called Golgotha.

At the base of the mountain, Abraham tells his porters and servants, *"Stay here with the donkey; the lad and I will go yonder and worship, and we will come back to you"* (Gen. 22:5). He tells them that he and the boy are going to the top of the mountain to *worship;* and after they finish, they'll be back down.

Get the picture: God says to take the boy up the mountain and slay him, burn him on an altar. And Abraham tells his porters, "We're going up the mountain to worship, and when we come back...." But if Abraham was going to be obedient and slay Isaac, then how could he plan to come back down the mountain with Isaac?

When they got to the top of the mountain, there was a dialog between Abraham and Isaac:

> *But Isaac spoke to Abraham his father and said, "My father!" And he said, "Here I am, my son." Then he said, "Look, the fire and the wood, but where is the lamb for a burnt offering?"* (Genesis 22:7)

Where is the lamb? The paradigm for worship is in this text. This passage is the model, the blueprint, for worship. Isaac asked, "How can we worship without the sacrificial lamb?" The same question is raised in our day: How can so many people and religions "worship" without consideration of the Lamb, the Messiah, God incarnate? It is amazing how often that which is supposed to be worshiped takes place with no thought of Jesus as both the perfect sacrificial lamb and the object of worship.

"Where is the lamb for the burnt offering?"

Abraham replies in the next verse to Isaac's poignant question: *"My son, God will provide for Himself the lamb for a burnt offering"* (Gen. 22:7).

The word rendered "provide" in the English is the Hebrew source of the name of God, *Jehovah Jireh,* which means "the Lord will provide" or "the Lord who provides." The Hebrew also implies sight and perception as in "to gaze" or to "look on" or "to see."[5] Thus, the Lord who provides is the Lord Jehovah Jireh—the Lord who sees.

The Latin compound for the word *provide* comes from two words: the root for our word *vision,* which is the Latin *vide* (from which we get our word *video*) and the prefix *pro. Vide* means "to see." *Pro* means "before." How is God our source? By being our sole provider. How does He *provide*? By having *prevision*; He sees what's coming before it gets here. *He sees the need before it's a need.* The God who hears your prayer, not only heard your prayer before you asked it, but He sees the answer to your prayer before you see it.

> *Then they came to the place of which God had told him. And Abraham built an altar there and placed the wood in order; and he bound Isaac his son and laid him on the altar, upon the wood. And Abraham stretched out his hand and took*

the knife to slay his son. But the Angel of the Lord called to him from heaven and said, "Abraham, Abraham!" So he said, "Here I am." And He said, "Do not lay your hand on the lad, or do anything to him; for now I know that you fear God, since you have not withheld your son, your only son, from Me" (Genesis 22:9-12).

God provides the provision as an overflow of worship through the relationship that acknowledges Him as our source and as our Master. In the case of Abraham and Isaac, here is what God's *"prevision"* provided:

Then Abraham lifted his eyes and looked, and there behind him was a ram caught in a thicket by its horns. So Abraham went and took the ram, and offered it up for a burnt offering instead of his son. And Abraham called the name of the place, The-Lord-Will-Provide [Jehovah Jireh]; *as it is said to this day, "In the Mount of the Lord it shall be provided"* (Genesis 22:13-14).

The passage says that a ram was caught in the thickets; his horns were caught in the bushes. The text implies that Abraham was told to look. When he looked, he saw the ram already caught. It was not a miracle ram; God did not say, "Let there be ram," and—*bam!*—a ram. The text implies that the ram was there by the time Abraham looked, which means that the ram was there before Abraham got there.

Remember, Abraham went up the mountain to worship. When he got there, he looked around and there was already a ram, caught in the bush. Chronologically, the ram would have had to come up a different side of the mountain from the one which Abraham and Isaac climbed. The animal would have had to arrive in time to already be stuck in place when Abraham and Isaac got to the place of the sacrifice. This means that the provision for the sacrifice got there ahead of Abraham's need of it.

If Abraham had turned around and had not gone to the top of the mountain as God instructed him, or if he had refused or had done a halfway job, he never would have seen the ram, which was the provision of God, who was Abraham's source. The answer and the provision were already waiting for Abraham to show up with his need.

All Abraham had to do was to be obedient to stay on the trail, walk by faith, and walk in the things that God said until he saw their fulfillment. God was his provider—and He provided *in advance.*

The provision had been scheduled by God to arrive in perfect time: God time.

God Provides Before You Ask

I declare to you that *God is your source.* He has provided for you everything that you need to fulfill the vision to which He has called you. The destiny, the call, the picture that God has given into your spirit--everything you need--is already in place in the spirit realm. It is *already done.* God is not waiting for you to get there so He can do it; God has already provided, because He is your source. Your challenge is to stay on the road and walk by faith and do everything He tells you to do. Walk in obedience, keep trusting God, and not worry about what you see along the way. Keep your eyes on Him and don't listen to people who tell you that you aren't this or you aren't enough of that or you don't have the right stuff or you don't know enough of whatever. Learn to ignore the naysayers.

People aren't your source. But the God who *is* your source has already made a way, so that when you do what He says, you will get to exactly the place He wants you to be. He makes a way where there was no way; if you can just hold on and stay on the path and not listen to people who would drag you down, your provision is already there with your name on it. It's up to you to follow His path so you can get it.

It cannot be stated enough: God always provides before the need arises! He sees our needs before we ask. Our biggest challenge is to walk by faith, fully believing what God says. The challenge comes down to making a decision as to whom we are going to believe: God or our circumstances. Will you trust God or your critics? Is your faith in the God who says you can, or in those who say you cannot?

The provision is already there, waiting on you to make a decision. The need is already met. You may take a winding road up the mountain, but the text implies that *Abraham never stopped.* If you are tempted to stop because it hasn't happened yet, keep in mind that you just don't see it yet. Don't stop because you're struggling. Struggle onward, reminding yourself: "But God said."

Have you ever had nothing to hold onto but *God said?* Hurdles, stoppages, storms, blockages—but *God said.* Sometimes that is all you have to hold on to. It does not make sense. There's no logic to it. But *God said.* There will be times in your life when that is all you have to hold onto. It will be those times when the enemy Mammon will step in and try to entice you with alternative sources.

One day, I was talking with a woman who was about to get married. She shared with me what a challenge it had been for her trying to live holy as a single mother after a very tragic and bitter divorce. I had seen this woman try and struggle to walk upright as a woman of God. I had seen her weep because of no social life. I had seen her tempted by very wealthy men, men of resources who would pay to spend time with her, who would set up a chain of events that would lead them to the bedroom with her. Yet, I've seen her stay holy, stay on the path. I've seen her cry because men made fun of her commitment to God. I've seen her struggle when men tried to cause her to fall in the eyes of God. I've seen when her discernment uncovered these men and revealed them for who they really were.

Not long ago, she came to me with both a tear and a twinkle in her eye, and introduced me to the man she was about to marry. Her God provided all of her needs, because He is a provider. He had provided the answer before she got there. She was tested along the way, to make sure she got the lessons God wanted her to get. But she stayed the course. And she received her provision from God.

I've seen His provision in my own family. My daughter Jessica came to me one day, telling me that she had to take a certain test for a class at the university she was attending. I wanted to encourage her as she struggled to prepare for the class, so I said, "Why not drop this class?" She said, "Daddy, I have to pass this test in order to take the next class." It was a required class. If she planned to graduate, she had to pass the required classes—they were not optional.

God is testing many of us in these present days, not because He's angry with us, but because He's preparing us for the next class. He will provide everything that you need to be the man, the woman, the marriage, the career, the servant of God that He has called you to be.

Your challenge is to settle two things in your heart right here and now:

1. God is my source.

2. I will stay on His path; I will put my life in His hands.

Abraham said, "I'm going up, and I'm coming down." His words and behavior implied, "I walk in obedience. Therefore, I will offer my son. If I offer my son, he will die. Yet, if I go up that mountain and worship Him, I will come back down and my son will have lived. How can both can be true? Only if God performs a miracle. Only if God steps in. So Abraham pulled out his knife (because you slay the sacrifice before you offer it) and was about to thrust the knife into Isaac. And the angel said, "Hold it, hold it! Wait, Abe! That's far enough. Now I know your heart. You passed the test."

Why would the angel stop Abraham before he slayed Isaac? *Because Abraham had already slain the boy in his heart.* He had already obeyed God in his heart. In his heart, Isaac was dead. *God honored his heart.*

Sometimes I pray to God, "How are You going to pull off this one, Lord?" In my mind, I can't make sense of it. But my heart is right. In my heart I want to obey Him. In my heart I want to please Him. So I take my life and all that I am and I put it in His hands. And by faith I say, "Make whatever You want to make out of it."

As clay to the potter, I surrender myself into the hands of my Master and say, "Shape me, O Lord; mold me and make me. Make me the man You want me to be. Make me the pastor You want me to be. Make me the husband You want me to be. Make me the father You want me to be. I don't know how You're going to do that out of this mess, but I place all of it in Your hands." And the potter takes that clay—that life—into His hands and works it.

Sometimes, of our own will and our intent and our own bents, that which God is making in His hands becomes distorted. We made bad choices and became weak along the way and blew it and are headed down the wrong path, and this clay in His hands could potentially become something other than the kind of artistic masterpiece that He intended. In those cases, here is what God does not do: He doesn't take the clay and throw it away. He doesn't leave my clay and start working on somebody else. He takes the clay that's headed in the wrong direction and He pounds on it...and He shakes it...and he molds on it...and He pounds it down...and He starts all over again.

I cannot tell you how many times He's had to start over with me. I can't tell you how many times I have felt the loving yet chastening pounding as God reworks in me a humble submission to Him.

And then He builds me back up.

I place my life in His hands. I trust Him that much. I can't make it make sense. But I trust Him. He has a perfect plan for me. *That's worship.* Trust Him. He'll teach you to see your life through His eyes.

Don't let that devil Mammon fool you, trick you, trip you up, or try to convince you he has a better plan for your provision. Look to God and to God only as your source. In Him, you live and move and have your being (see Acts 17:28).

All that you need is in Him.

Endnotes

1.   Alexis de Tocqueville, *Democracy in America, Volume II* (New York: D. Appleton and Co., 1904), 716, http://books.google.com/books?id=KO8tAAAAIAAJ &printsec=frontcover&source=gbs_v2_summary_r&cad=0#v=onepage&q= &f=false (accessed November 22, 2009).

2.   In Genesis 16, Abraham had another boy, Ishmael, who was born before Isaac. In her impatience to hurry along God's promise, Sarah had requested that Abraham sire a child through her maidservant Hagar. Ishmael was conceived outside of the will and direction of God. Therefore, during Abraham's test, God referred to Isaac as Abraham's only son. God was saying, "Take the son *I* gave you, not the one born of Sarah's maidservant."

3.   *Biblesoft's New Exhaustive Strong's Numbers and Concordance with Expanded Greek-Hebrew Dictionary.* CD-ROM. Biblesoft, Inc. and International Bible Translators, Inc. s.v. "olah" (OT 59030).

4. Isaac wasn't a little child when this occurred. He was as old as perhaps his late teens to early twenties, and as young as 13 or 14. He was no tiny tot. He was a young man.

5. *Biblesoft's New Exhaustive Strong's Numbers and Concordance with Expanded Greek-Hebrew Dictionary*, s.v. "ra'ah" (OT 7200).

Notes

Chapter Six

MAMMON AND THE HEART

On that night God appeared to Solomon, and said to him, "Ask! What shall I give you?" And Solomon said to God: "You have shown great mercy to David my father, and have made me king in his place. Now, O Lord God, let Your promise to David my father be established, for You have made me king over a people like the dust of the earth in multitude. Now give me wisdom and knowledge, that I may go out and come in before this people; for who can judge this great people of Yours?" (2 Chronicles 1:7-10)

IN the passage above, God appeared to Solomon and told him to ask of Him whatever Solomon wanted. It is as though God gave him a spiritual blank check. Solomon cashed that "check," asking God for wisdom and knowledge to effectively lead God's people.

God saw that Solomon's heart was right and responded by honoring Solomon's request:

Because this was in your heart, and you have not asked riches or wealth or honor or the life of your enemies, nor have you asked long life; but have asked wisdom and knowledge for yourself, that you may judge My people over whom I have made you king—wisdom and knowledge are granted to you; and I will give you riches and wealth and honor, such as none of the kings have had who were before you, nor shall any after you have the like (2 Chronicles 1:11-12).

God said, "Ask!"

Solomon replied, "I want wisdom and knowledge so I can be an effective leader of Your people."

God responded: "Because the pre-eminent concern and priority of your life is the Kingdom and My call on your life, I'm going to give you what you ask. I'll give you wisdom and I'll give you knowledge—and I'm going to give you some things you could have asked for, but didn't: I am going to give you riches, wealth, and honor."

Because Solomon's heart was set on the Kingdom God had given him, God granted him more than he requested; He gave Solomon riches, wealth, and honor. The word *honor* in this context simply suggests fame or a reputation reflective of one's riches. In other words, God promised to give Solomon honor among men because of the blessings evident in his life.

First of all, God affirmed that He is the source of riches and wealth. He is the one who bestows them. Second, the text indicates that there is some difference between *riches* and *wealth* (a distinction we will explore later), because God told Solomon, "I'll give you both." This is not a redundancy on God's part.

Look closely and you will see that something is missing in this promise of God—something that we assume is there, but actually is not. God says, "I'll give you riches. I'll give you wealth." He does *not* say, "I'll give you money."

In our culture—in *most* cultures—there is an assumption that riches or wealth (or both) include money. However, as we will discover, there is a difference between riches and wealth—and money isn't even on the agenda.

What is the difference? Before we answer that question we must first remember this: Whenever issues are raised involving finances, money, material blessings, and possessions, there is a release of the demonic force or entity known as *Mammon*. This is true in regard to our passage from Second Chronicles, because the text is talking about wealth. Wealth includes finances and material blessings; therefore,

Mammon (whose assignment it is to influence and impact our attitudes toward finances, money, material blessings, and possessions) rises to attack.

It's also important to remember the three ways in which we can respond to the blessings of God: We can operate in a spirit of pride (demean the blessings by taking credit for them or by exaggerating our worthiness of them). We can respond with a spirit of poverty (demean the blessing and apologize for being blessed). Or, we can respond with a spirit of gratitude (acknowledge that we have been blessed purely because God is our source). The correct response, of course, is an attitude of gratitude.

When God blesses us, He releases blessings from the spirit realm and manifests them in the earth realm. The source is God Himself.

Two Systems

Jesus said you are in the world but you are not of the world. You must understand something about every blessing that you receive in the earth realm: this world system is under the control of the evil one:

> *We know that we are children of God, and that the whole world is under the control of the evil one* (I John 5:19 NIV).

Solomon said that his concern and his heart were for the Kingdom. As Christians, you and I are blessed within the workings of the world system because, although we are in the world, we are not *of* the world. There are two kingdoms identified in this dual "universe"; they are the kingdom of darkness and the Kingdom of Light (or the kingdom of the evil one and the Kingdom of God). The two kingdoms operate under two totally different principles, discussed briefly in Chapter Three:

- The Kingdom of God operates under a system of *giving and receiving.*

- The world operates under the strategy of *buying and selling*, a system of commerce.

They are two completely different systems.

God was saying to Solomon, in effect, "Your heart is with the Kingdom of God. Therefore, I will give you the type of riches and wealth that can be received by a Kingdom mind-set of giving and receiving." Because God gives us freedom of choice during our time on earth, it was Solomon's decision that determined which system would be the guiding principle for his life.

Solomon was about to receive from God riches and wealth. He had to choose whether he would use them in the world system, (applying the mores and values of the kingdom of darkness) or in the system governed by the Kingdom of Light.

God promised Solomon riches and wealth, but made no mention of money. So what, then, is wealth? Deuteronomy 8:18 says: *"You shall remember the Lord your God, for it is He who gives you power to get wealth. . . ."* The text is not saying that God gives you the power to get money. The difference can best be explained by going to the biblical example in Genesis.

In Genesis 13:2, we learn that the first man officially designated as being rich was Abram: *"Abram was very rich in livestock, in silver, and in gold."* The word for "rich" in this text is the same word rendered "honor" in the verse where God told Solomon that He would give him riches, wealth, and honor (see 2 Chron. 1:12). Honor is related to glory, the *chabad* of God (the weightiness or heaviness associated with Him).[1]

In essence, God was telling Solomon, "I am going to honor you with the weight of material blessings." The phrase "very rich" in Genesis 13:2 means that Abram was honored by God. Here's how he was honored: he had cattle, silver, and gold. Thus, *wealth is that which has intrinsic value because it was created by God.* Abram was wealthy, rich, favored, and blessed in livestock, silver, and gold. Solomon was wealthy because he possessed something that *only God makes.* He had something that had inherent value because it was made by the Creator of the universe.

You don't make gold, or silver, or cattle; only God does. In Genesis 15:18 God said to Abram, *"To your descendants I have given this land. . ."* so that Abram was wealthy in livestock, gold, silver, land, and eventually children. The person who is wealthy is that person who has in their possession that which only God can give. In making a covenant with Abram, God said, "Part of the covenant is that I'm going to bless you with children." This was a promise to which God was so committed that He made it when Abram was too old to have children. All the children he was going to have would have to start with a single child produced despite the limits of Abram's physical capacity. In other words, any child of the greatly aged patriarch would have to be produced by the miraculous power and ability of God.

But that wasn't all. God added, "Not only am I going to bless you with a child you could not produce at this stage of your life, but I'm going to bless your child and his generations—your grandchildren, great-grandchildren, and so on. Plus, I will bless the world through your family, because I'm a God who is establishing a covenant that is bigger than you." (This is the Abrahamic covenant spoken of in Genesis chapters 12, 15, 16, and 17 by which God promised to bless Abraham and his generations and the world through them.)

Wealth is that which has intrinsic value because it was created by God. In Psalm 50:10 God says, *"The cattle on a thousand hills* [are Mine]." In Haggai 2:8 He says, *"The silver is Mine, and the gold is Mine."* God not only created gold and silver and cattle, but it's all His. Wealth is that which you are to transfer to your children, from one generation to the next. Abraham is the model; from his life we learn how God's people can be honored with the weight of wealth, riches, and honor.

Why then does God give us, as Deuteronomy 8:18 says, *"the power to get wealth"*? The answer is found in the rest of the verse: *"that He may establish His covenant which He swore to your fathers, as it is this day."* He gives us the power to gain wealth so that He might affirm His covenant. His covenant is not just designed to bless you; His covenant was given so that He would bless other people through the blessings that He gets to you. (I'm not talking about money yet; we're still talking about wealth.)

Thus, *wealth* has trans-generational potential. Wealth affirms God's covenant. When the Bible says, in Proverbs 13:22, that a good man leaves an inheritance for his children's children, God is speaking of *wealth*. The term "children's children" always takes us back to the Abrahamic covenant. It reminds me that the essence, the ultimate value, the productivity, of my life cannot be evaluated during my lifetime. It continues to be evaluated during the lives of my children's children. God affirms His covenant with me through my children's children, whom He blesses through me.

Money Versus Wealth

In Matthew 22, the Pharisees tried to trap Jesus on the issue of taxes:

> *"Tell us, therefore, what do You think? Is it lawful to pay taxes to Caesar, or not?" But Jesus perceived their wickedness, and said, "Why do you test Me, you hypocrites? Show Me the tax money." So they brought Him a denarius. And He said to them, "Whose image and inscription is this?" They said to Him, "Caesar's." And He said to them, "Render therefore to Caesar the things that are Caesar's, and to God the things that are God's"* (Matthew 22:17-21).

Why was the coin Caesar's? It was his because it was minted by his realm and had his image stamped on it. Therefore, Jesus told them to render the coin to Caesar.

Jesus also said to render to God the things that are God's. This means there is a distinction between what Caesar owns and what God owns: whatever it is that Caesar owns must be governed by Caesar's rules. *Money is merely a medium of exchange.* It is a means of exchange for products, goods, and services.

For example, you work for a designated period of time, and then you expect your pay. You work because someone hired you to render a certain amount of service or produce a certain number of products. In exchange for your work (your labor, time, and effort) you are given money. You then exchange that currency for the goods or services you need or desire.

Money operates in the earth realm. Money has no value in Heaven. Money operates solely under the world system. The world system is under the control of the devil.

How Wealth Opens the Door to Mammon

We know that money is not wealth—wealth is created by God; money is created by man. However, wealth can be rendered into money.

For instance, when man takes silver or gold or copper or bronze or nickel out of the ground and then mints it, God's created wealth is transformed into currency (often bearing the stamp of a ruler or nation). That which began as wealth that only God can create has now been transferred into a medium of exchange that facilitates the buying and selling of products, goods, or services in the world's system.

Whenever we take the created resources of God and monetize them (turn them into money), we transfer wealth out of the Kingdom of God and into the kingdom of man. Once that transfer occurs, the resources come under the dominance of the enemy who controls the world system.

The wealth you have is backed up by a "gold standard" that only God creates. Yet, once that wealth is converted to currency, it is subject to the rules and laws of a world dominated by the devil.

Remember, *wealth is that which has intrinsic value because it was created by God*. Thus, for example, land is wealth, silver is wealth, livestock is wealth, human beings are wealth, etc. At the point when these God-created things are converted into money (i.e., exchanged for currency) is when that wealth has been monetized (a "cash value" placed on it, so to speak). In other words, we don't take a chunk of land or a bar of silver to the grocery store and exchange it for a quart of milk and a loaf of bread. But we can sell the land or gold for currency ("money"), and then take that currency to the grocery store to exchange for goods.

Monetized wealth (wealth converted to money) makes the assigned corresponding monetary value of the item much easier to see, to handle, to conceptualize, to use and manipulate. In other words, in our culture we visualize the "value" of a piece of land more quickly if we see a money "price tag" on it than we do when seeing the raw land in front of us.

Money opens the door to Mammon, the demonic spirit to whom satan has assigned the task of influencing how you will handle the wealth God has given you (whether or not it is turned into currency).

A great biblical account of wealth being turned into money is seen in Luke 15, the story of the prodigal son.

> *A certain man had two sons. And the younger of them said to his father, "Father, give me the portion of goods that falls to me." So he* [the father] *divided to them* [his sons] *his livelihood* (Luke 15:11-12).

The younger son asked for his portion of the father's estate. His father granted his request, turning over to him his share. After the son squandered it all, he found himself in dire straits; he was living in a far country, well below the standard of living he enjoyed in his father's house.

The money the young man spent was gotten when he sold the parcel of property (the land), which represented his portion of the inheritance. The instant the wealth (his land) was turned into money, Mammon stepped in and helped to convince him to squander it on partying and wild living. One version says he spent it on *"riotous living"* (KJV); another version says he wasted it *"on parties and prostitutes"* (TLB); a third version says *"he squandered his estate with loose living"* (NASB). Once wealth is turned into money, the enemy rises up!

Abraham's story was quite different. The Bible says that God blessed Abraham with relationships—people, sons, daughters, grandbabies, family—because *that's what wealth is.* If you want to see what happens when wealth is turned into money, watch a family when somebody dies and leaves a little money. Too often, when the survivors of the deceased conclude that the wealth resulting from that relationship has been turned into money, they start lining up at the front door to get their share—and some of them you don't even know! I have seen families go crazy and fall apart when there is money to be had.

Suppose good ol' Uncle Bud died and happened to own a farm down in Louisiana and he left it to a loved one. That farm is wealth; but once the inheritor sells the farm and converts it into cash, that money is subject to the attack of Mammon. It is governed by the rules of a world dominated by the enemy. This is why inheritances that start out as great blessings are so often whittled down to nothing in no time at all.

When wealth becomes money, it is subject to the attack of Mammon.

Mammon and Relationships

Mammon influences the value we place on money. When we exchange money for goods, products, or services, it is the spirit of Mammon who quantifies the transaction and puts a price tag on it.

This is especially true in terms of relationships. For example, you may feel that the services you offer are worth the price of your rent or your car payment. But remember, once wealth has been transferred to money, it becomes an easy opportunity for the enemy to step in and mess with. Likewise, once a relationship has been reduced to how much money you pay me, what bills of mine you take care of, what you buy or don't buy from me, you have reduced a human relationship that only God can give, down to how much money you owe me, how much money you pay me, and how much money I give you. You have "monetized," "dollarized," a relationship given to you by God. A price tag has been put on it; and now that relationship between two human beings is operating under the ways of the world system, in the same way that a corporation operates a profit-driven endeavor. It has become all about the *money.*

When a relationship comes under attack for whatever reason, Mammon steps in and exploits the situation, planting seeds of bitterness, anger, and revenge. Before you know it, "I'll see you in court!" is being shouted in anger, because a price tag has been put on a broken heart. All too often, money becomes the tool or weapon by which couples get back at each other. The money extracted from a spouse in court is the price they're paying for whatever they did to break their mate's heart.

Mammon prowls everywhere. He runs a large division of the army of the devil. He oversees the attempted monetization of every single physical possession on earth, including people. When anything God made is reduced to a monetary value, Mammon steps in.

So how should we handle that? How do we relate to money, to material blessings—especially when they present opportunity for the enemy to attack us? First, realize that money itself is not evil, as Paul taught:

> *For we brought nothing into this world, and it is certain we can carry nothing out. And having food and clothing, with these we shall be content. But those who desire to be rich fall into temptation and a snare, and into many foolish and harmful lusts which drown men in destruction and perdition. For the love of money is a root of all kinds of evil, for which some have strayed from the faith in their greediness, and pierced themselves through with many sorrows* (I Timothy 6:7-10).

It is the *love* of money that is evil. The next two verses go on to say: *"But you, O man of God, flee these things and pursue righteousness, godliness, faith, love, patience, gentleness.* ***Fight the good fight of faith***..." (I Tim. 6:11-12).

The "good fight of faith" is not so much about general spiritual warfare; it's the fight that you enter into to stand before God in righteousness and godliness based on how you handle money. You fight the fight of faith based on how you handle money and blessings.

The good fight of faith involves those who are able to be blessed and still stand holy. Still remain righteous. Still be godly. Still walk with humility. Know that you have to bless somebody else to be a channel of blessing to others—to be able to be blessed and still pass on something to bless your children with, to realize that all that you have comes from God, who is your source, and to give Him all the glory and honor and credit. The Bible says all of that is a struggle—a *fight*. How we handle money is a fight of faith. We are not to succumb to the obsession and the passion of *"money money money money."* God alone is our source. He never blesses me for me, but that I might turn around and bless somebody else. That's godliness, that's righteousness, that's Christlike, that's spiritual and holy.

The fight we fight is a fight of faith *over material blessings*. That's the context of this passage from First Timothy. The fight of faith is not about binding and loosing the devil. The fight of faith is when you bind him off of your finances, your bills, your mind-set, and your attitude toward blessings, and then turn around and give God all of the glory because you realize that He *alone* shall supply all of your needs.

Now, that is a fight! It's a fight against principalities and powers, tendencies and bents, whisperings and enticements of the demon, Mammon, and the ways of the world system that he has his claws in.

For many people, the more God blesses them, the farther away from Him they get. What would you do if God gave you one million dollars right now? I'll tell you: you would do the same thing that you would do with the last $100 bill in your pocket. Most people would do the same thing with whatever money comes in later as they have done with the money they have already had.

God knows your heart. Remember what He told Solomon, "Your heart is right, My son." God wants to bless you, but He wants you to grow enough to learn how to handle His blessings. Can you stand to be blessed? Can God trust you with wealth? Can He trust you with riches? God's ultimate concern is not about the size of your bank account, *it's about the size of your heart*.

I've seen married people with money whose marriages have crumbled. I've seen poor people whose marriages have crumbled. It's about your heart. It's about understanding that God simply wants to make you a channel of blessing. It's about keeping your priorities straight. Solomon's desire was for God's Kingdom, for wisdom and knowledge so that he could be an effective leader for God's people.

Is your heart with God's Kingdom?

Endnote

1.   *Biblesoft's New Exhaustive Strong's Numbers and Concordance with Expanded Greek-Hebrew Dictionary.* CD-ROM. Biblesoft, Inc. and International Bible Translators, Inc. s.v. "kabad" (OT 3513).

Notes

Chapter Seven

WEALTH AND PROSPERITY

A good man leaves an inheritance to his children's children, but the wealth of the sinner is stored up for the righteous (Proverbs 13:22).

THE Bible uses at least five economic terms in relating to and speaking of both the economy of the Kingdom and the economy of this world. The Bible talks about wealth, money, riches, prosperity, and treasure.

As we learned in the previous chapter, *wealth* speaks of that which has intrinsic value, a value that comes from God. Psalms 50:10 says that *"the cattle on a thousand hills"* belongs to God. This speaks of God as the owner in the context of livestock. One of the ways in which wealth was measured in ancient times, was by the amount of livestock and cattle a person possessed. Another form of measurement was assessed (and is assessed today) in terms of precious metals. Haggai 2:8 quotes God as saying, *"The silver is Mine, and the gold is Mine."* The precious minerals that God placed in the earth are a universal form of wealth.

It all began when *"God created the heavens and the earth"* (Gen. 1:1). Land is also considered a measure of wealth. It is a finite commodity because God is not making any more land. He has already created the heavens and the earth. Over the centuries parcels of land have passed from owner to owner, but the combined acreage of these parcels remains virtually unchanged.

The same God who created the heavens and the earth also made man and then gave him woman. So now we know that *wealth includes both the tangible and the intangible.* It includes all that God makes (tangibles such as land, livestock, animals, and creation). It also includes intangibles, such as relationships between people. Since God is the one who makes people and puts them together on the earth, relationships are a measure of wealth. A person is counted wealthy if he or she is involved in healthy relationships.

We have all seen people who have a lot of money, yet are miserable. Likewise, we know people who are blessed with loving relationships and experience an intangible form of wealth that has nothing to do with money or material riches.

Proverbs 13:22 makes clear that wealth can be found in the hands of the world and, specifically, in the hands of sinners. The God who owns all the wealth does not necessarily *control* all the wealth and money. Although God owns *everything,* He also partners with us in the use of wealth and money and other resources here on earth—even to the point of allowing us control over many things. Yet, He still *owns* it all (while no doubt desiring that we will handle it properly). As we covered in the previous chapter, wealth can be transformed into money. Once this transformation occurs, that money (which was not created by God) and is possessed and controlled by people, moves out of the Kingdom of God.

"Render unto Caesar that which Caesar owns," Jesus said (see Matt. 22:21; Mark 12:17; Luke 20:25). He was referring to a coin made of metal that came from the earth but was subsequently formed into a medium of exchange (which is what all money is). Jesus said that money bears the image of its owner, and that His disciples should render that money to its owner, specifically Caesar. Jesus' words imply that Caesar is symbolic of the world system—the system under which all money (wealth that has been transformed into the currency) is governed.

Proverbs 13:22 says that a good man leaves an inheritance for his children's children. In the context of the verse, the word *inheritance* refers to a place, or something to be occupied. When God says to leave to your children's children an inheritance, it means you are to leave them space to occupy.[1] The word speaks of land that is divided. We've already learned that God owns all the land (as a part of the wealth He created). God says that a good man leaves an inheritance. Space, a place, land, is to be occupied by the children's children.

This verse also says that the wealth of the sinner is "laid up" (KJV) for the righteous, or the just. The term *laid up* denotes being covered for protection. This wealth is covered or protected. It is being kept *on reserve*, by the sinner who is laying it up for the righteous. It is wealth that is currently under the control of the sinner and the "world system."

One implication of this text is that the world knows how to handle the wealth even more so than the saints of God do (see Luke 16:8). This is wealth that is under the control of the enemy, the world, the unrighteous people and God-rejecters who don't realize that they are controlling and holding onto this wealth as a sort of "layaway" for the righteous.

Certain department stores and other establishments allow people to put purchases on a layaway plan. When I was growing up in St. Louis, we used to buy everything on layaway. "Dollar down, dollar a week." This meant that you could choose something from the rack, and because you said you would buy it eventually, they would take the merchandise out of circulation and hold in the stockroom for you. When your weekly payments were finished and the merchandise was paid in full, the goods were yours to take home.

Likewise, God says the wealth of the sinner (that is, the wealth of the world system) is controlled by them but not owned by them. It is only being held on reserve in the "stockroom"—it's on "layaway," for the righteous.

How Do We Get It?

The question is, *how do we get it?* How do we obtain that which sinners are unwittingly storing up for the righteous of God's Kingdom? We know it's on layaway for us, but we haven't been told how we can redeem it.

First of all, you must understand that if it is under the control of the world's system, you must play by the world's rules. In other words, you cannot go and just name it, claim it, frame it, in the name of Jesus. You can't just blab it and grab it, and call it yours. That's a good shout, but it won't get you your blessing.

The world system works under a different principle than the Kingdom system does. The world system, as we have learned, works under the principle of buying and selling. The Kingdom works on the system of giving and receiving. Nobody is going to give it to you, and you can't steal it. But there is a way to appropriate that which is laid up for you if you are one of the righteous.

God says that He gives you power to get wealth, and you do that by playing by the worldly rules governing commerce, money, and financial affairs—just as long as, once you get it, *you then transfer it from the kingdom of the world to the Kingdom of the glory of God.* Your power to get it, then, is to play by the world system of buying and selling; and you do that with *money.* The idea of God giving you the power and ability to gain wealth means that He gives you the resources you need to function in the system that is controlled by the world. But it only controls that which God has destined to be transferred back into the Kingdom of Light.

Joshua 24:13 says:

> *I have given you a land for which you did not labor, and cities which you did not build, and you dwell in them; you eat of the vineyards and olive groves which you did not plant.*

In other words, God says He's going to give us power, (remember, Deuteronomy 8:18) ability, and resources, to get land and possessions that we did not "build," but which have been on layaway for us.

Through the use of the resources He releases into our lives, there will be a wealth transfer from the kingdom of the world to the Kingdom of our God. When we take control of it, we will, for the most part, be taking control of land, houses, and things God said we did not create. They are on layaway for us, waiting until the transfer occurs.

As a saint, a believer in the Lord Jesus Christ, every time you buy property, a house, a building, you transfer that asset from the kingdom of darkness to the Kingdom of Light. Every time you complete one of these transfers, you are using the power He's given you to get wealth—through the earth system of buying and selling.

An example of this involves the church where I am senior pastor. We are in a facility that we did not build. But God decreed this building, which had been on unwitting secular layaway for us, to be released to the Kingdom of God. When we bought it, we didn't just buy a big sports arena; we made a transfer of something that was built in the world system—for us. We transferred the asset at God's appointed time. Now it is in His Kingdom, and we are occupying it.

Today, that famous sports arena is sanctified, made holy, consecrated by the presence of the living God. God owns it. The wealth that was in the hands of nonbelievers, secularists, the unrighteous, was on "layaway" for the just and the righteous who now own the building. Yes, it is used during our off-hours, so to speak, for conventions and ball games and concerts. In other words, "the world" rents our building and pays us to come in and use it (and they pay as very well, too). Every time they pay us, more wealth that would have been recycled into the world is being transferred into the Kingdom of God. All of this is by the providence of the living God who gave us the wealth to buy the Los Angeles Great Western Forum sports arena.

Understand that *money is nothing more than a medium of exchange involving goods and services.* When wealth becomes money, it then becomes part of the medium of exchange in the earth realm. There is no power in money itself. There is no authority in it. It is amoral. Money is not the root of all evil. It is the *love* of money that is at the root of much of the evil of the world.

> *"War seldom enters but where wealth allures."*
> —John Dryden, *The Hind and the Panther*

Be Faithful

It is important to be fearless in believing that you can financially step up as you follow God's laws. If you are counted among the righteous, if you've learned to handle money God's way, if you use it as a tool and not as a possession to hoard, if you are willing to work hard, if you prove yourself trustworthy to be a conduit to pass God's blessings on to others, then just watch and see if He won't begin to transfer the wealth of the unrighteous over to you.

This is not a *pie-in-the-sky, sit-back-and-wait on the world to give you something* entitlement mentality. This is a faith that trusts God to give you power (which is added to your labor) to gain an income, to get and hold a job, to develop creative ideas, so that He can establish His covenant of blessing you and blessing others through you.

> He who is faithful in what is least is faithful also in much; and he who is unjust in what is least is unjust also in much. Therefore if you have not been faithful in the unrighteous mammon, who will commit to your trust the true riches? And if you have not been faithful in what is another man's, who will give you what is your own? (Luke 16:10-12)

This brief passage is a succinct parable about stewardship. If you have not been faithful in that which belongs to another man, then who is going to give into your care anything truly valuable? Jesus was saying that if you have not been faithful with that which is least (*least* in the context of this parable refers to money, which, in the eyes of God, is a little thing), if you have not handled money wisely, if you haven't been trustworthy, if you've been unfaithful in handling unrighteous Mammon, in dealing with the demonic force that urges you how to handle money, He asks, then how can you be trusted with true riches? If you have not handled well that which belongs to another person, how can you expect to receive that which is being held in trust, so to speak, for you?

This verse implies that there must be *two kinds of riches.* Jesus wasn't talking about the money that God owns. He's already clarified that money belongs to the world system. Common sense would tell you that if you handle what is yours the right way, you qualify to get more for yourself. But that's not what Jesus is saying. Remember, *money is but one of the tools by which God blesses and empowers His people.* It is a tool by which God measures our commitment and spiritual relationship with Him as well as our level of trustworthiness in handling material blessings from Him. It is a tool that facilitates the proclamation of the Gospel by God's people. Acts 1:8

clearly states that we *"shall be witnesses to* [Him] *in Jerusalem, and in all Judea and Samaria, and to the end of the earth."*

By Book or by Crook?

I've got a news flash: it costs money to get the Gospel out to the world! The devil knows the potential that you have in different areas of your life by how you handle money. He evaluates your potential to build an inheritance for your children's children. He monitors your progress as a living demonstration of the power and truth of Almighty God. He gauges your potential in spreading the Gospel.

Aware of your potential, the devil has several schemes by which he unleashes Mammon like an attack dog sent to arrest your progress. First, he wants to make sure that you get as little money as possible. Second, if he can't stop you from making it, he's still not finished; he will attempt to mess with your mind and distort your value system so that, if you get money, he will entice and cleverly convince you to mismanage it.

The enemy Mammon attacks our minds and influences the way we handle God's blessings. He tries to keep those blessings out of our control. He wants to make sure you miss payments, misspend your money, misunderstand the fine print on the loan document—all tricks to destroy your credit. One of the ways Mammon will attack your handling of money is to get you over your head in debt. If all of your resources are used to pay interest, you have nothing left with which to bless anybody.

God's intention is never for you to get finances for yourself only; His desire is for you to receive blessings, be blessed by them, and then pass them on to others. If you are so far underwater that you are overwhelmed by debt and even bankruptcy, you won't be able to bless anybody, because you will have already *unblessed* yourself.

Riches

The Bible talks about another word: *riches.* Your paycheck is money you work for; you put in time and you receive wages in exchange for your efforts.

Riches have to do with *money that works for you.* Riches take you into the area of overflow. If you have riches, you have enough to pay all your bills, meet all your obligations, have all your needs met, and still have resources left over. Riches relate to those "spendable," or expendable, end-resources that go beyond your needs and into the purchase of conveniences and luxuries.

Most of us would define the rich as those who have enough money to live an abundant life whether they work to earn their money, don't work at all, or stop working altogether. *Once you have more than you need, you become a target for the enemy*—and he never lets up. If your excess is not earmarked for creating wealth or inheritance, it becomes subject to the attack of the god, Mammon. If it is not set aside, designated, clarified as *this is what it's for,* and marked for use in building more wealth for the Kingdom of God or for building an inheritance for your children's children, then riches become part of the bulls-eye that's like fresh meat to the jackal, Mammon.

Matthew 19:16-22 and Mark 10:17-22 tell the story of a rich man who asked Jesus what he must do to have eternal life. Jesus told him to take all of his riches and give them to the poor. (We'll examine this story in detail in the next chapter.) The Bible says that the man walked away sorrowful, because he was rich and had many possessions. The danger of the attack of the enemy Mammon on the overflow of our lives is that he will try to convince you to trust in your riches, in your investments, in your "financial portfolio," rather than in the God who allowed you to get into financial overflow in the first place.

God does create millionaires. On the one hand, there are many Christian "millionaires in training"—not because they're so super-spiritual, but because they will sit under the Word of God and honor Him and get into a position to where He can trust them with overflow blessings. On the other hand, if Christians are being financially blessed "above and beyond" by God, but they mess up and mishandle their blessings, they are subject to being "taken back to school" to relearn what they may have forgotten about God's ways.

George Thompson, pastor of stewardship at our church, is gifted in the area of financial management. God has used him to train men and women how to handle financial blessings. During the economic crisis of 2008-2009, more than 20 families in our church lost their homes. Through the ministry of the Word, by the will and way of God, and through instituting godly principles of financial management, almost 30 homes were saved—right in the middle of those times of economic famine.

What About Prosperity?

Prosperity is a word that goes beyond wealth, beyond money, and even beyond riches. Let me tell you what many of the saints have done: Because of the preaching of extremist positions and extreme theologies that have distorted the issue of prosperity, many have thrown out sound Bible truths and closed their minds.

That attitude, which is encouraged as another one of the countless deceptions "massaged" into the Church today by Mammon, causes many people to miss out on the financial blessings God wants to bring into their lives.

God does not so much talk about giving us money; He talks about causing us to prosper. In fact, the word *prosper* does not even include money. God says He will make your way to prosper (see Josh. 1:8). God says He will do this if you meditate upon the truth of His Word. Then you shall make your way prosperous and you shall be a success.

Etymologically speaking, the word *prosperity* is related to the word *succeed*.[2] To succeed and be prosperous means this: God will clear the path and He will take you on your journey; He will be with you so that you achieve what He desires and arrive at the ultimate point of the journey on which you have ventured.

To prosper means that you *succeed to the point of excellence* or to the highest level. God has said that He will bless you with everything that you need to not only start your journey to the top of the mountain, but to mount every crest and navigate every valley until you arrive at the highest point—the success God has ordained for you.

God wants you to prosper in everything; therefore, He wants you to prosper financially. *God wants you to be as wealthy as He has ordained you to be.* You have a responsibility to be all that you can be in the areas of finances, money, material blessings, and possessions, because God has given you certain gifts to get you there.

Let's assume, for the sake of discussion, that He has provided you with academic preparation, a mind and intellect with which to think and reason, and other gifts designed to bring financial rewards. What happens if you are too lazy to get up and go to class and too undisciplined to do your necessary studies? What if you desecrate the gifts God has given you? The answer is simple: You are choosing to live beneath that which God has ordained for you.

God has blessed you to be prosperous, which means that on the journey of your life, He has called you to be the man or woman that He wants you to be. Approaching it from the other direction, if you are a prosperous Christian who desires to do the will of God, then you will also want and strive to be all that He wants you to be. When we settle for less, we are dishonoring God, who has given us the potential for more so that we can give to those in need. If we settle for less, we have dishonored God, who says we can do all things through Christ who will strengthen us (see Phil. 4:13).

You cannot allow the enemy to stop you. You cannot allow people to stop you. You cannot allow naysayers and "haters" to stop you. They are not your source; in discouraging you, they are playing into the hand of the enemy. *"Greater is He that is in you, than he that is in the world"* (1 John 4:4 KJV).

God has called you to excellence. He has called you to succeed. He has called you to stand on the mountaintop and declare that you got there by nothing but the grace of God. He has not called you to mediocrity. You cannot allow Mammon to infect your thinking in negative or self-destructive ways where finances, money, material blessings, and possessions are concerned. My daddy always told me to do and be the best that I can. He never said "be the best," he said, *"do"* your best!

Make Your Life a Testimony

Some people have a testimony—not because they've been so good, not because they've been so faithful, not because they've been so kind, but because God led them up the mountain. Every time the devil threw an obstacle in their path, God either took them around, over, or through it.

A testimony is when Mammon attacks your financial situation, but you trust God and hold on to Him through hell and high water. God wants us to be an example of His blessings. He wants us to be prosperous in how we conduct money matters. He wants us to view prosperity through His lens, which means seeing who we are in Him without consideration of what brand of car we drive, what size house we own, what style of clothing we wear, or how much money we have sitting in a bank account.

God has given every Christian something on the inside that will hold us when the storms of life are raging, when the enemy is railing, and when Mammon comes roaring. God has given you something on the inside that will let you walk with your head high because you are a child of the King of the universe. Just as surely as He will teach you and test you on the lessons, He will also bless you.

God's plan and desire is to prosper you (see Jer. 29:11). Prosperity is bigger than money. Prosperity is more than a paycheck. Prosperity gives you things that money cannot buy. With money you can buy a house, but money can't buy you a *home*. A home is created by relationships with loved ones, and God alone makes people and gives relationships into your life. With money you might buy a car, but money can't buy you safety in your travels. Safety has to do with the presence of God along your journey.

God says He will make your *way* prosperous. Your way is *a journey*, a place you are going as you proceed from one place to another. Progress is part of your journey. That's why you can be prosperous before you get the money you need to buy what you need. You might even be low on cash, yet you have great favor and things are provided. Favor is another form of prosperity.

Some people haven't got a dime, but they've learned how to keep their heads high and their dignity intact while God works His plan. They know that His plan will bring blessing into their lives in His perfect timing. These are people who walk not by sight, but by faith (see 2 Cor. 5:7); they are people who have learned to call those things which are not as though they already were (see Rom. 4:17). They've learned to look past the phony enticements of Mammon and focus on the authentic blessings of God. Prosperity rises up in their spirits saying, "There's something on the inside bigger than what people see on the outside."

God does not say He'll give us money, He says He has given us the ability to get wealth, and that as we follow His ways, we will enjoy prosperity (which comes from what we do with wealth). Wealth and prosperity are things that only God can make. When I follow Him and when I use the ability He gave me to gain wealth, then I will have wealth that can be converted into money to provide for my needs and to give to others to help with their needs. I can leave an inheritance for my children's children. I can help my neighbors.

It is no problem whatsoever for God to transfer wealth from the hand of the sinner and from the world monetary system into the Kingdom of His glory. He does it through His followers.

God wants us to understand that if we have not learned how to handle finances, money, material blessings, and possessions properly, in His ways, then we are in a position where *we cannot be trusted with true riches.* Learning and maintaining a proper perspective on principles involving these blessings positions us to not only be good stewards of God's monetary blessings, but to be channels of blessing to others *and* helps us to recognize and avoid the pitfalls of the devil, Mammon. How we deal with the things Mammon has been assigned to upset, to distort, to control, and to make us misunderstand, is an indication of how much God will be able to trust us with things of lasting substance, with things that matter most, with "God wealth"—the *true treasures.*

Endnotes

1. *Strong's Dictionary,* "nachal" (H5157), *to occupy, to leave for;* "nachalah" (H5159) *an estate, inheritance.*

2.   *Merriam-Webster Online Dictionary.* Merriam-Webster Online 2009, s.v.
     "prosper," <http://www.merriam-webster.com/dictionary/prosper>
     (accessed: November 23, 2009).

Notes

Chapter Eight

True Treasure

Do not lay up for yourselves treasures on earth, where moth and rust destroy and where thieves break in and steal; but lay up for yourselves treasures in heaven, where neither moth nor rust destroys and where thieves do not break in and steal. For where your treasure is, there your heart will be also (Matthew 6:19-21).

An actor on TV was talking about movies and about making sequels. He said that the challenge with sequels is that they are rarely as good as the first movie in the series. He added that the best sequel of all time is the *New Testament*, the scriptural "sequel" to the Old Testament.

He's right. The Bible is a book of history that records the journey of the people of God and the progressive revelation of the person and character of God. The Bible contains prophecy that pulls back the veil of time and speaks of things that are not, often as though they already were. The Bible is a book of biographies that lifts up men and women, flaws and all, as examples of the goodness, grace, and mercies of God.

Interestingly, the Bible is also a book of economics. It's a book that lays out Kingdom principles of economic progress and principles that speak to the people of God in the *now*, while also teaching eternal consequences. As we learned in a previous chapter, the Greek word *oikos* is a word that is built on the root for the word *house*. From the word *oikos* comes the word *oikonomia*, which speaks of the management of a house, and is the root of our English words *economy* and *economics*.

In the biblical sense, *economics* simply means "the management of a household." You and I, as citizens of God's Kingdom, have a choice: we can operate and manage our lives, homes, and affairs according to Kingdom principles, or according to principles of this world. How we manage and run our houses is, etymologically speaking, related to the biblical concept of economics, which relates to the topics of money, riches, finances, and material possessions.

Get It Before It's Gone

Paul Samuelson and William Nordhaus wrote a very popular economics textbook titled *Economics*.[1] Many institutions of higher learning use the book. In it, Samuelson and Nordhaus provide an interesting definition of *economics*. To paraphrase them, Samuelson and Nordhaus say that economics is the study of how people and societies choose to employ scarce resources that could have alternate uses, in order to produce various commodities and distribute them for consumption.

What Samuelson and Nordhaus are saying is that economics involves the handling and management of scarce resources by the world's societies. This includes how those societies utilize their scarce resources to produce products and commodities for distribution within a given society.

The operative idea behind the management of a household or economics in the world system is based on the assumption that you are managing *scarce resources*. The world system assumes that there is only so much to go around. This idea is antithetical to the philosophy of God's Kingdom, which talks over and over about abundance, overflow, and prosperity. You and I can choose to operate our lives and our households from the philosophy of the world, which assumes scarcity (and presumably a dwindling) of resources. Or we can operate from Kingdom philosophy and principles, which assure us that everything God has for us will be there at just the right time.

The world system operates on a zero-sum formula that says there's only so much to go around. Therefore, if you *have*, someone else *has not*. Likewise, if you *gain*, someone else must *lose*. Every time you become covetous of what belongs to somebody else, you are shifting into the world's mind-set.

The Kingdom of God does not operate on a zero-sum principle that says in order for you to be blessed, someone else has to get hurt. You don't have to struggle to "get yours" before someone else takes what is yours. That is anathema to the very heart of God. He does not bless you at the expense of someone else. The Kingdom of God says that there is sufficiency and abundance, and that everything God has ordained for you is yours. No one can get what God has purposed for you and assigned to you.

For example, if it's God's will that a woman get married, the economy of God would never advocate taking someone's husband and giving him to her. That's a world mind-set, a "mammonic" system of thinking, so to speak. The Kingdom mind-set says that God shall supply all of our needs and He'll supply them from out of His riches, not from out of somebody else's bedroom.

Before we examine the connection between economics and *true treasures*, let's do a quick review of some of the terminology we have learned so far:

- *Wealth*—Something that has intrinsic value as created (and thus owned) by God. The cattle on a thousand hills belong to God; silver and gold belong to Him; land, air, and the whole earth all belong to Him (see Ps. 24:1). Wealth consists of all of those things that man cannot create. Wealth is amoral, is not good or bad in itself (the issue is how it is used).

- *Money*—A medium of exchange created by man. Jesus said, *"Render unto Caesar what is Caesar's"* (see Matt. 22:21) and He used the illustration of a coin with Caesar's image stamped into it. The system of money is only used in the domain of man and the world system. Money is created when man takes God-created wealth and converts it into a tangible medium of exchange for goods and services. For example, to the extent that the gold standard backs up American dollars, that creation of that money is based on something that was originally created by God. Money is amoral, neither good nor bad in itself (the issue is how it is used).

- *Riches*—Riches consist of money at work. Riches go beyond your working for money; riches involve money that is now working for you. Riches can work for good or for evil. From the Kingdom mind-set, riches can become a tool or slave for God or for the devil.

- *Prosperity*—Prosperity goes beyond money, wealth, and riches. Prosperity is related to the word that comes from *road* or *way*, which means that God makes your way blessed, He gives you favor on your journey.[1] He assures, through prosperity, that you achieve and arrive at the destination of your journey. Prosperity has to do with your becoming everything that God ordained that you would be. This includes fulfilling God's ordained purpose for your life and being blessed by God with favor on your journey. Your path will not be obstacle-free, but God grants you the grace, mercy, power, and authority to advance beyond every obstacle and fulfill His calling for your life.

Treasures

Now we come across a new word: *Treasure*. In Matthew 6:19, Jesus said, *"Do not lay up for yourselves treasures on earth...."* Apparently, we have a choice as to where we will store up our treasures. Jesus didn't say that we shouldn't lay up (or store) treasures. He was not emphasizing the topic of having things. The emphasis here is more about locality than about substance.

Jesus said we should *be mindful about where we lay up our treasure*. We are not to lay up treasure on the earth; He said to lay it up in a different location, which is Heaven (see Matt. 6:20). The warning (actually stated as a commandment from the Lord) indicates that, just as there are two places to store up treasures, there are two kinds of treasure: worldly treasure (treasure in the earth realm) and true treasure (treasure in the Spirit or heavenly realm).

In the economy of Jesus' earthly days, wealth was measured in terms of coins and land and livestock—and also quite often in terms of one's wardrobe. Back then, wealthy people were known to change clothes three or four times each day. It was a display of wealth, because clothing was part of one's wealth.

Jesus said in Matthew 6:19, however, that their clothing was susceptible to the attack of moths. Not long ago, I was getting ready to preach and my wife thought I had a spot on the back of my jacket, so she started flicking at it to try to get it off. She quickly realized, however, that it wasn't a spot; it was a hole that had been eaten away by a moth. It happened to be a suit that I'd had custom made while on a trip to South Korea. In fact, it was one of my favorite suits. There was no other suit like it—I know, because I picked out the material and designed it myself. And now my nice suit had a hole in it, eaten away by moths. Have you ever tried to patch up a moth hole? It's not that easy. Don't lay up treasure on earth, where moths can eat it.

You also don't want to lay up treasure on earth, where rust can destroy it. When I was in the eighth grade, I bought a necklace for a girl. It was Christmastime, and I wanted to give her something beautiful. So I went to Woolworth's, bought the necklace, and wrapped it with a nice little bow. I put a love note inside the box and gave her the gift right before Christmas break.

From the moment I gave her the gift, I looked forward to January, when school would start again. I was so excited about the prospect of seeing her wearing my little gift. On the first day back at school, I noticed that her neck had a tinge of a green, crusty ring around it that she was scratching. I did not understand how my treasure from Woolworth's could have turned that girl's neck green. Be careful with treasure that can rust!

Your treasure is that to which you attach a high value. Whatever you esteem, covet, want, crave, like, enjoy, want more of, that is your treasure. We are not to lay up for ourselves treasures on earth, because earthly treasures are corruptible. Jesus did not speak against possessing things, nor did He say not to enjoy them. He said that in this corruptible, decaying, finite physical dimension called earth, material possessions are susceptible to deterioration and destruction. They are temporary and will fade away. By contrast, everything in Heaven is incorruptible and enduring.

You get to define what your treasure is, but Jesus made it clear that wherever your treasure is, your heart is going to be with it. He warned us not to put our trust in stuff, in things, in material possessions. We are not to become attached to a level of materialism that is self-seeking and binds us to this world.

I grew up in East St. Louis, Illinois, just across the Mississippi River from St. Louis, Missouri. When I was a little boy, I noticed that all of the "big" preachers drove Cadillacs. I thought Cadillacs were the coolest cars. However, I also noticed that hustlers and dope dealers also drove Cadillacs. (That's another story for another time.)

The movie *Cadillac Records* is about the rise and fall of Chess records, one of the most successful record labels in the 1950s. Its recording stars included the likes of Muddy Waters, Chuck Berry, Etta James, and countless others. One of the ways Leonard Chess became so wealthy was by paying his artists by giving them Cadillac cars.

There is a scene in the movie where Leonard Chess, the owner of the label, introduces blues man Muddy Waters to the label's new artist, Howlin' Wolf. (I love these names!) Mud points at his shiny Cadillac and says to Wolf, "Welcome to Cadillac Records. Stay around long enough and everybody gets one."

Howlin' Wolf pats his old beat up pick-up and responds, "This ole truck, I own it. It don't own me." Howlin' Wolf knew where to put his treasure, and he knew where his heart was.

Muddy Waters asks Chess, "Any royalties come from my song 'Hoochie Man'?"

Chess answers, "I already gave that to you."

"How you figure?" Mud replies.

"Cadillac ain't free, Mud," Chess tells him.

The scene closes with Muddy saying his wife wants a house. Chess says, "I'll take care of it." He bought the house Muddy lived in—and gave Muddy the Cadillac.

It a tragic turn of events, the harmonica-playing blues man, Little Walter, was killed in a fight over a crap game. When he died, he was broke. His closest friend, Muddy Waters, had been paid in Cadillacs and didn't have any money, either. Mud had to go to Leonard Chess to ask him to pay for Little Walter's funeral. All of Muddy's "treasure" was in the Cadillacs.

In this passionate scene, Howlin' Wolf flashes a big wad of money and says, "I'm lookin' to help bury a fellow musician," indicating that he had a heart of compassion to help pay for the funeral of a colleague, and that his treasure was not in the car he drove. His treasure was in the right place because his heart was in the right place.

There are instances, however (such as in Luke 19:11-26), when Jesus commended those who were entrusted with money to make wise investments. Again, this indicates that His admonition about treasure was not a condemnation of having things. Rather, it was a warning that putting your trust in material items will result, not in your possessing stuff, but in *stuff possessing you.*

Jesus said, "Don't lay up *for yourself* treasure on earth, but lay up *for yourself* treasure in Heaven." Notice who controls the treasure: You determine what the treasure is; you lay it up for yourself; and you decide where you want to lay it up—in the earth or in the Kingdom of God. But remember, wherever you choose to lay up your treasure, that's where your heart will be also.

It would seem as though the treasure would follow your heart, your cravings, your desires; but that's not what the text indicates. The text implies that your heart will follow whatever you define as treasure. If you want to know where your heart is, find out what your treasure is. What is it that you highly value? Whatever that is, that's where your heart will be. The object of your desire (your treasure) will reveal your heart and expose your loyalties.

For example, one evening some time ago I was in Philadelphia, speaking at a conference. My heart, however, was in Los Angeles, because that's where my treasure was (my wife, my kids, my grandkids, my church). It was a challenging time of ministry because my head and my heart were in L.A. To paraphrase the song popularized by Tony Bennett, "I left my heart in Los Angeles" (I know; Tony says San Francisco). My heart was there because my treasure was there. I struggled to concentrate on my message. I had been traveling a lot, and probably should have stayed home with my treasure! But my struggle was based on the principle that where your treasure is, that's where your heart will be.

Our treasure determines where our hearts are. If you want to find your heart, don't go looking for it; look for your treasure. Wherever you've put your treasure, your heart will be right there with it.

What do you treasure? What is your heart following? Is it things of this earth? Is it the things of God, the things of Heaven? The choice is ours, we have the power to tell our hearts what to follow. Deciding where to put your treasure is a challenge, because it forces you to establish your priorities and governs your handling of your life, your household, your blessings, and your finances.

If your treasure is in Heaven, your heart is in God's Kingdom.

What God Wants With Our Treasure

Now as He was going out on the road, one came running, knelt before Him, and asked Him, "Good Teacher, what shall I do that I may inherit eternal life?" So Jesus said to him, "Why do you call Me good? No one is good but One, that is, God" (Mark 10:17-18).

This man came to Jesus and called Him *good.* Jesus challenged the man's evaluation of Him. He corrected the man, saying that the only one who is good is God. There is an important cultural application to this reference: in those times, to deem a person as being good was to imply that you were submitted to that person's goodness. It meant that you would follow whatever they said and believed that, whatever they asked you to do, it was right. You were essentially pledging your submission and obedience to that person.

Jesus continued, saying,

> *You know the commandments: "Do not commit adultery," "Do not murder," "Do not steal," "Do not bear false witness," "Do not defraud," "Honor your father and your mother"* (Mark 10:19).

The young man responded, saying, *"Teacher, all these things I have kept from my youth"* (Mark 10:20).

Verse 21 tells us that Jesus looked at the man and loved him. The chronology of the text implies that, because Jesus' loved the man, He was about to make a request of him. In fact, He was about to challenge the man to the very core of his heart. And because the man had already said Jesus was good, Jesus *expected to be obeyed.*

Here's the flow of the scene: The man wanted to know from the "good Teacher" Jesus, what he must do to inherit eternal life. Jesus questioned the man's use of the word *good.* The implication from Jesus is this: *We'll see if you're really interested in inheriting eternal life.* Still, Jesus loved the man and answered his question, saying, *"One thing you lack: Go your way, sell whatever you have and give..."* (Mark 10:21).

In this verse, the Greek translated "give" is *didomi.*[2] A Hebrew word for "give" is *nathan.*[3] Whether in Greek, Hebrew, or even Aramaic and Syriac tongues, the word *give* has a simple meaning about which there can be no doubt. Surely the rich young ruler in this Bible passage understood the implications of what Jesus told him to do. So, let's review the story, from the perspective of Jesus' implied thoughts toward the man:

- You called Me good, therefore I assume that you will obey Me.

- I love you.

- Because I love you, I am going to challenge you. You want to know how to enter the Kingdom and how to operate your life with a Kingdom mind-set. So here's My challenge to you: "Give to the poor, and you will have treasure in Heaven."

Jesus said, "Don't lay up treasure for yourself in the earth realm, but lay up treasure in Heaven." Now He tells the young man (and us, specifically) how to deposit, and create treasure, in Heaven: *"Sell whatever you have and give to the poor, and you will have treasure in heaven."* Take what you have and go sell it and give the money to the poor! An action like that for a man who has spent a lifetime amassing treasure on Earth will indicate without a doubt where his heart really lies.

Jesus affirmed utilizing the world system for a Kingdom cause. Remember, the world functions through a system of buying and selling. Jesus told the man to take what he had and convert it into money (sell it) and then give the money to the poor. Buying and selling is the operative system of the world; it is a system of Mammon, a system influenced by the fallen angel called Mammon. The man told Jesus, "I've kept all of the commandments." In other words, "I'm already religious." In our culture we might say: "I go to church every Sunday," or "I'm in the choir," or "I'm a deacon," or "I'm on the usher board."

But Jesus responded, "You're missing something. If you want to know how to have eternal life and enter the Kingdom—you have to realize that you're missing just one thing." Jesus wanted the man to understand that the things he had done would not get him treasure in Heaven.

There was more to this than just the mechanics and the outward things—as important as those are. What he lacked was something that would have touched his heart. The only way to lay up treasure in Heaven is to give. Jesus' words *". . . give. . .and you will have. . ."* implied by verb tense that the man would have treasure in Heaven, effective immediately.

To whom should we give?

To the poor, to people in need.

How does God record my giving in Heaven?

Jesus said by our giving to the poor.

Why is that significant?

It is significant because Jesus said, *"The Spirit of the Lord is upon Me, because He has anointed Me to bring good news to the poor. . . ."* (Luke 4:18 NRSV).

My friend Steve Harvey says, "The best thing I can do for the poor is to not be one of them."

That's not arrogance. Steve has a good point: if you are poor and have a need and I have no more than you do, how can I bless you? You gain treasure in Heaven when you regard others with the character and nature of Christ. You gain treasure in Heaven when you value the lesser-off, when you sow into their lives, when you touch their lives, deposit into their lives. You gain treasure in Heaven when you share with others in need that which God has given you. God says that all of those things don't go in your "portfolio" here on earth, but into your account in Heaven.

One of the most selfish spiritual attitudes we can ever have is to ask God for just enough to get by. This is different from Solomon's asking not to have so much that he would forget God; or so little that he'd turn to ungodly means as stealing and disparage God's name. This is an attitude of, "Lord, I don't want much. I don't need much. Just give me enough to meet my own needs." It is not a spiritual attitude, it's a selfish attitude, because you cannot bless other people if you only have enough for yourself.

Jesus has enough for everyone. He has enough to get it to you and get it through you to others who are in need. That's His heart; receive from Him and sow into somebody else's life—then you will be depositing treasure in Heaven.

God Wants *Givers* Who *Trust*

Over the past couple of decades, we have been so contaminated by an extreme prosperity gospel and theology in which the emphasis is on getting more stuff for ourselves. The emphasis has been on what God wants to do for you and what God has for you. You've heard me call these teachings "name it, claim it, and frame it" and "blab it and grab it." This kind of theology has nothing to do with God and everything to do with self. It has bred a generation of self-centered, narcissistic, selfish, arrogant people whose intention is not to turn around and bless others. This extremist theology misses the very point of blessing.

Jesus told the rich man, "Where you missed it, young man, was that you decided it was all for *you.* You're not willing to trust it into My hands so that I can bless you as you bless somebody else. What you don't realize is that I want to keep on blessing you so that you can keep on blessing others!"

The man was operating under the zero-sum philosophy of the world which says there are limitations and there is a scarcity of resources. The Bible says he walked away, grieved at the Master's instructions, *because he couldn't let go of his possessions* (see Mark 10:22). The man's great wealth had him in a death grip. He could not bear to share.

Jesus knew that if the man gave away all he had, he would then have to trust Jesus as his sole source of provision. Jesus did not just say, "Go and sell it." He said, "Sell it and follow Me." This would require a paradigm shift for the man: instead of trusting in his wealth, he would have to learn to rely on Christ to meet his needs.

Here's the interesting thing about the exchange between Jesus and the rich man: After the man left, dejected at the admonition to get rid of everything and replace himself as provider with Christ as his provider, Peter and the disciples freaked out. They were worried that, if salvation was all wrapped up in how much we have, nobody would make it into Heaven! Matthew 19:25 says, *"When His disciples heard it, they were greatly astonished, saying, 'Who then can be saved?'"* In Matthew 19:27, Peter said, *"We have left everything to follow You!"* (NIV).

Let's return to the account in Mark's Gospel, with an eye to examine Jesus' words to His "astonished" disciples:

> *Then Jesus looked around and said to His disciples, "How hard it is for those who have riches to enter the kingdom of God!" And the disciples were astonished at His words. But Jesus answered again and said to them, "Children, how hard it is for those who trust in riches to enter the kingdom of God! It is easier for a camel to go through the eye of a needle than for a rich man to enter the kingdom of God." And they were greatly astonished, saying among themselves, "Who then can be saved?" But Jesus looked at them and said, "With men it is impossible, but not with God; for with God all things are possible"* (Mark 10:23-27).

The key, Jesus said, is in where you put your trust: is it in riches or in God? The issue is not whether you have it or not; it's where you put your *trust*. He was saying that you cannot go into the Kingdom if you are trusting in the things of this world.

The disciples got pretty upset. They were not a bunch of down-and-out broke misfits. Peter, a successful fisherman, said, "We've left everything and followed You" (meaning, obviously, that they'd left everything in terms of their hearts, their attachment to the world; Peter could not have left everything material, because after Jesus was crucified, Peter went back to his fishing business).

Mark 10:29-30 records Jesus' response:

> *Assuredly, I say to you, there is no one who has left house or brothers or sisters or father or mother or wife or children or lands, for My sake and the gospel's, who shall not receive a hundredfold now in this time— houses and brothers and sisters and mothers and children and lands, with persecutions—and in the age to come, eternal life.*

Jesus addressed eternal matters, but notice what is missing from this list: *there is no mention of money*. This is because money is not the issue. Houses are built on land that God made. Relationships (the prototype being Adam and Eve) and all the human beings involved in them are from God, too. What God is saying is that everyone who has left *wealth* for His sake and the Gospel's sake, will receive it back a *hundredfold*.

Multiplication, Not Addition

The principles of the Kingdom are diametrically opposed to the operative principles of the world. Jesus said we are not to lay up treasure in the earth. The world system operates on buying and selling; worldly financial investments grow by addition and by percentage of interest. But the Kingdom system operates on *multiplication*. When you see phrases in the Bible such as "thirtyfold," "sixtyfold," and "a hundredfold" (as in Matthew 13:8, for example), they are always in the context of a biblical, spiritual principle. The Kingdom does not operate by addition, but by multiplication.

What God is saying is crucial: When you make a deposit of treasure in the earth, the best return you can get involves some addition and a percentage of interest. But when you deposit a treasure in Heaven, it grows exponentially, by multiplication.

It's time to shift in our mind-set. It's time to go to another level. It's time to learn another principle of life. Every God-inspired sacrifice that you make is validated, blessed, and multiplied by the Kingdom principle. Jesus said you make deposits of treasures in Heaven when you give to others with the character and nature of Christ—when you give to those in need.

Be Content: It's Not Over

I rejoiced in the Lord greatly that now at last your care for me has flourished again; though you surely did care, but you lacked opportunity. Not that I speak in regard to need, for I have learned in whatever state I am, to be content...
(Philippians 4:10-11).

To be content is not the same as being complacent. Paul lived by a Kingdom principle; he learned to be content no matter what situation he was in. His contentment is not to be confused with a state of apathy or acquiescence to difficulty. To be content means this: "I know God has something down the line and I'm satisfied where I am. I know I'm not going to stay here; He's going to get me there in His good time. I know this thing is not over yet. I know what God promised me. I know that He who has begun a good work in me will not stop until He completes it. So I know that wherever I am, if it's short of where God said I'm going, it's alright because I know I won't be staying there forever. I trust Him and I have faith in Him."

That is the essence of being content.

Be content wherever you find yourself, because you're not going to stay there. The journey is not over. God is not done with you. He began something in you and He will perform it until He completes it. In the end, He will get the glory. So don't freak out; don't give up; don't get depressed; and don't throw up your hands, because *God is not finished yet!* You are not where you are going to be. God is a God who lives and dwells beyond the *now*.

Later in his letter, Paul told the Philippians that they had been a blessing to him:

> *Nevertheless you have done well that you shared in my distress. Now you Philippians know also that in the beginning of the gospel, when I departed from Macedonia, no church shared with me concerning giving and receiving but you only* (Philippians 4:14-15).

Paul was saying to them, "You are partners with me because, by giving and receiving, you are involved in the ministry that I'm involved in. I've sown into your life and you've sown into my life."

In today's vernacular Paul might have said, "I'm not begging, guys, because I know that God chooses the channel through which He'll bless me. And if He has to, He'll surf the net and simply change the channels of my blessing. God has used you Philippians as a channel of blessing to me, and I want you to know it has not gone unnoticed. When you gave to me, it was credited to your account in Heaven" (see Phil. 4:17).

God says that when you give to the furtherance of the Gospel, you are creating an account in Heaven with your name on it. So that when you give and when you sow into a place where the Gospel is going forth, or when you give to someone who is struggling, or to a cause that uplifts the Kingdom of God, or into a place where lives are being changed for the good, God records it on His ledger of your spiritual portfolio in Heaven. It is "added to your account."

In Luke 16:9, Jesus said, *"I say to you, make friends for yourselves by unrighteous mammon, that when you fail, they may receive you into an everlasting home."* This verse means that Kingdom people learn how to use the system of the world. Jesus said that to make friends using your money is to utilize it and the resources of this world as instruments or tools to touch lives for the Kingdom.

This is not talking about buying friendships; it is talking about putting money and resources to work, making them your slaves in accomplishing God's will on the earth. Then, when "earth money time" is over and the systems of the world economy, life in the flesh, and worldly exchange fail...when you get to the end of your journey and arrive in Heaven, you will have greeters there. They will be the people who got there because of the way you handled your money and helped the Gospel to touch their lives, save their souls, take them to glory! They will be in Heaven because of your Kingdom mind-set and the investments that you made while on earth.

Who are some of the people who will be in Heaven because of the seeds you planted into their lives? Look around you: Who is in your church now that wasn't there a few years ago? Who came in after you began to give to a ministry or to an outreach? These are the ones who are there because of your generosity. They are saved and learning and growing in their walk with Christ!

It is absolutely essential that we learn to understand the flow of Kingdom dynamics, the way God's system works, the way He blesses through people who bless others. This is why Paul said in Second Corinthians 9:7 that *"God loves a cheerful giver."* He's not into people who give grudgingly or because they were told to give. Remember: in Mark 10:21, Jesus affirmed that He loved the rich man *before* He asked him to give to the poor. In the economy of the Kingdom, money is nothing but a tool through which the Gospel is released and saves souls from hell.

Paul told the church at Philippi: *"Even in Thessalonica you sent aid once and again for my necessities"* (Phil. 4:16). Recently in just the span of a few months, I was able to go to South Africa, London, and the Ukraine to minister. I was able to go because some of the members of Faithful Central Bible Church—many who have never been outside their own city—sowed into the ministry. Leaders were strengthened. Souls were saved. The downtrodden were encouraged, uplifted, and blessed. Marriages were strengthened.

We developed a relationship with an AIDS ministry in South Africa. Most of the members of the Faithful Central Bible Church congregation will never go to South Africa. But they are now represented there because they used worldly resources for a Kingdom cause. All of this happened because of some folks at church who operate in the Kingdom principle of blessing others and ignoring the spirit of Mammon.

The Kingdom mind-set is one that realizes that *all we have comes from God*. And when He speaks to us to release what we have to those in need, we obey. We don't grieve, like the rich man did who said he obeyed all of the commandments, yet refused to follow Christ's advice.

I pray that we Christians become a people who never care more about our own "stuff" than we do about God's heart for the needy, the broken, the poor, and the downtrodden.

True treasures are not found in the earthly realm. Yet, we can choose to use the riches of the world in ways that lay up treasures in Heaven—*and stop Mammon's work cold.*

Endnotes

1. *Economics*, Paul Samuelson and William Nordhaus, McGraw-Hill Publishers, 2001.

2. For an in-depth discussion on prosperity, see Chapter 10 of my book *Making Your Money Count* (Regal Books; 2007).

3. *Biblesoft's New Exhaustive Strong's Numbers and Concordance with Expanded Greek-Hebrew Dictionary.* CD-ROM. Biblesoft, Inc. and International Bible Translators, Inc. s.v. "didomi" (NT 1325).

4. Ibid., s.v. "nathan" (OT 5414).

Notes

Chapter Nine

GOD'S CIRCLE OF BLESSING

He who sows sparingly will also reap sparingly, and he who sows bountifully will also reap bountifully. So let each one give as he purposes in his heart, not grudgingly or of necessity; for God loves a cheerful giver. And God is able to make all grace abound toward you, that you, always having all sufficiency in all things, may have an abundance for every good work. As it is written: 'He has dispersed abroad, he has given to the poor; his righteousness endures forever.' Now may He who supplies seed to the sower, and bread for food, supply and multiply the seed you have sown and increase the fruits of your righteousness. . .
(2 Corinthians 9:6-10).

IT is the mission of Mammon to get our focus off of God's track and distract us from His purpose for the use of money in the world. Mammon was to get us on his track, the secular world's system of understanding and utilizing finances, money, material blessings, and possessions.

In the passage just quoted, Paul outlined five divinely ordered purposes of money for the believer. The context speaks of giving materially, or financially. In verse ten he spoke of our giving as being seed which we sow. He said that God is the one who supplies seed to the sower. Here are the five God-ordained purposes of money for believers in the world system:

1. To supply seed to the sower

2. To provide bread for your food

3. To multiply the seed that is sown

4. To use the seed to increase the fruits of your righteousness

5. To give

Paul began our passage by saying, *"He who sows sparingly will also reap sparingly"* (2 Cor. 9:6). Later, Paul wrote: *"God is able to make all grace abound"* (2 Cor. 9:8). So, we know that giving is a result of the grace of God. It is a "grace gift." It is the result of the release of grace on our lives that we give whatever we give.

When Paul said, *"God is able,"* He was speaking of God's continual ability. The Greek word translated "able" is *dunateo* (from *dunatos,* which means "powerful" and "capable").[1] The word is also related to the Greek word *dunamai,*[2] meaning "to be able or possible." In other words, God continually has the ability to release grace and power into the lives of His people.

Let's take another look at part of the passage from Second Corinthians 9. This time, we'll examine the connecting thread linking the following verses:

> *Whoever sows sparingly will also reap sparingly, and whoever sows generously will also reap generously. Each man should give what he has decided in his heart to give, not reluctantly or under compulsion, for God loves a cheerful giver. And God is able to make all grace abound to you, so that in all things at all times, having all that you need, you will abound in every good work* (2 Corinthians 9:6-8 NIV).

This passage indicates God's response to our giving is a release of favor. It's like a perpetual circle of blessing:

- God gives us grace to give...

- Our giving releases (or activates) grace in our lives...

- That grace produces the desire to give more...

- God gives us grace to give.

The word *bountifully* from the New King James Version of Second Corinthians 9:6 is an interesting word. It is really another form of the word for "blessing."[3] He who gives or sows as a blessing will receive blessings because he has blessed others. It's a circle of give and receive, give and receive.

He who gives a blessing will be blessed. Notice the contrasting statement from the same verse: He who gives sparingly, shall reap sparingly. It sounds like Paul was saying that if you give a little, you get a little; if you give a lot, you get a lot. But that's *not* what he said.

Sowing bountifully has a different spin than just that of giving much more. What Paul really said is that if you give or sow a little in a miserly, cheapskate sort of way, then the result will be lesser blessings for you. However, if you sow with the mind-set that giving is a blessing, then the result is more blessing back to you (in order that you would then give more).

This passage speaks of *how* we give—and that is determined by the heart. Therefore, the statement *"let each one give as he purposes in his heart"* (2 Cor. 9:7) shows that giving is never a matter of amount. The act of giving always surpasses the amount of giving and deals with the attitude that precipitates the amount. Giving is about the heart. God does not need your money. God wants your heart; for as we have learned, where your treasure is, your heart will follow.

The Bible says that God loves a particular kind of giver: the kind who gives cheerfully. It also says we are to give as we determine in our own hearts. Our hearts determine how we give, because people tend to give as an expression of what they treasure.

Notice what Paul said in Second Corinthians 9:7: *"God loves a cheerful giver."* The implication is that cheerful giving activates God's release of grace, because the next verse says: *"And God is able to make all grace abound toward you"* (2 Cor. 9:8). Are you seeing the linkage from verse to verse?

Let's look beyond verse eight to where Second Corinthians 9:10 says: *"He who supplies seed to the sower* [this is speaking of God, the one who administers seed and multiplies it at will]...*increase the fruits of your righteousness."* In other words, it is God's ability and desire to bless us. The phrase speaks of God's volition, His determined will. God wills to multiply it to us. God wills to increase blessings to us. God wills to bless us and to release grace to us. It all starts with cheerful giving, not grudg-ing giving.

God says He desires to bless His people. You don't have to manipulate God to bless you. You don't have to convince Him to bless you. We don't deserve it anyway! God does not give because you deserve *anything!* God gives because *He is a giver.* It's part of His nature to give. It's a part of the essence of His character. It is an outflow of His love for His children. He so loves that He gives (which is the example He sets for us to follow, as well). He can no more stop giving then He can stop loving. It's a part of His nature.

No Need for Any Other Source

The question is: *how do we handle that which God gives us?* There's a particular flow in the passage we are discussing. It says that God is able to make all grace abound toward us. It says that, having all sufficiency in all things, we will have an abundance for every good work. When you have all *sufficiency,* it means that you are without need of assistance. God, Jehovah Jireh, is not only our provider, but He provides without the need of assistance. He is our sufficient Provider.

God is able to make you sufficient, because *God Himself becomes your sufficiency.* It means that because of what He releases in your life, you have no need of aid from sources other than Him. In other words, you have within yourself all that you need (the Holy Spirit). He's able to release grace. Why? So that you might have all sufficiency.

God says it is His will that every need you ever have will be met in Him. God says that your relationship with Him is such that it is His heart's desire and his ability to meet every need you'll ever face. *It speaks of a psychological emotion of content-ment and satisfaction,* because you know that you will never face a need that God cannot meet. It speaks of an inner contentment. When God says, "all sufficiency," it means you're settled; you're satisfied. It means knowing that everything you will ever need is provided, because your source is God, who has the power to supply it.

The revelation is that God desires to be our source. The emphasis is on the fact that God is *able* to be our source. This is the subtlety of idolatry. Any time we look or expect anything or anybody else to supply a need, we've already desecrated our relationship with God, who says, "I'm the need-meeter here!"

Yet, there is a progression in this text. There is a movement from one degree to the next. His ultimate goal is not sufficiency, it is abundance. Watch the flow of the passage; it aims toward *abundance*, not mere sufficiency. It is the desire of the heart of God to be your sole source; and because He is your only source, you can rest peacefully, knowing that *He will meet all of your needs.* But He also wants to go beyond simply meeting your needs; He desires to bless you with abundance. It's the same God who transfers you from one level of relationship with Him to the next. As you get a grip on one, you move up to the next.

God's goal is not just to make you sufficient, but to make you *abound.* Why? So you are able to pour into the lives of those in need. *Abundance* means that you have over and above what you need. It means that you have more than enough. Abundance means providing beyond your needs. Abundance means there is an overflow. Whichever one of these definitions suits your fancy, just reach out and grab it. Whichever one registers with you, take it. They're all the same. They're all offered to us by God in His desire to bless our obedience to Him and our trust in Him.

I want to go for the overflow, personally. I want to live in the overflow of God. I don't want to live scrimping and scraping from day to day. I don't want to live begging and pleading. I want to get in a position where God moves me from sufficiency to overflow! Not for my own self-ingratiation, but because when I'm in the overflow, I'm in Kingdom territory, where He can use me as a channel to turn around and bless others in His Kingdom.

God Supplies Our *All*

Back to Second Corinthians 9:10: *"...He who supplies seed to the sower, and bread for food, supply and multiply the seed you have sown and increase the fruits of your righteousness."*

Watch the way apostle Paul divided up this verse: he said that God gives you seed for sowing and seed for yourself, which Paul called "bread for food." Bread symbolizes your need. So, He grants you seed for two different purposes: seed for sowing *and* bread for food.

Let's look at the latter: God does not make bread—you only get bread after you sow the seed He has given you (for your sustenance) and the seed brings forth a harvest. Once you harvest the seed, you turn it into flour and you bake your bread. That means God gives us everything we need to get the bread, but *we* have to initiate the effort to make it. There's a process to get from seed to bread.

The "catch" to this process is found in the word *supplies*. The King James Version uses the word *ministereth*. The New King James Version, the New Revised Standard Version, the New International Version and others use the word *supplies*. Still other versions, such as The Living Bible, use the word *gives*. The Greek word is *epichoregeo*,[4] from which we get our word *choreography*. The prefix *epi* means "upon," and the root word is similar to the word for choreography; it means this: "to supply the needs thereof."

Let's break it down.

God supplies. This word speaks of a person who is the conductor or sponsor or financer of a chorus that performs. It's a great picture of what happens in the artistic world, for example. It's like a troupe of performers. The one who supplies is the one who backs the troupe. Let's say it's a traveling road show, a troupe of singing performers who go from one place to the other. Somebody has to pay the bills connected with the performance, the traveling, the staging, etc.

In our analogy, the one who supplies the needs is God. He's in charge of all the details. When it's time for the actor or the performer to take center stage, everything he or she needs in order to perform their best has already been provided by God, who is working behind the scenes. The people out front see the "performance," but they never see God orchestrating, because He does so from behind the curtain.

Here's what God says: He is the supplier of the seed, which means that something has to happen in order for the seed to become bread. In our stage analogy, the actors are doing their part; but their center-stage work is only part of the process. Sure, the audience sees the finished product, the bread, so to speak. What they don't see is that someone has been working behind the scenes providing the means needed to turn a seed into a full loaf of bread—the complete performance of the show out front. That "someone" is God.

God's role behind the scenes of our lives—the making of the bread—is critical. Consider the following:

- *Somebody* has to tell the sower when to sow.

- *Somebody* has to prepare the ground to receive the seed.

- *Somebody* has to put the nutrients in the soil to receive the seed.

- *Somebody* has to tell the rain when to fall on the soil that was prepared to receive the seed.

- *Somebody* has to tell the owner when to pull the weeds from the soil.

- *Somebody* has to tell the soil when harvest time has arrived.

- *Somebody* has to tell the sower how much water to add to the flour and when to put it inside the oven and how long to leave it there and when to take it out.

God is orchestrating the entire seed and harvest cycle. All we see is bread on the table—but God has been working behind the scenes, every single step of the way. Isn't that just the way God works? He does His work behind the scenes of life.

People look at you today and all they see is the "bread," the results of God's "backstage" work. That work has been going on throughout the journey of your life up until now. They don't know what God had to put in place, or the kind of obstacles God had to bring you through. All they know is that you came out of the oven smelling good, in Jesus' name!

God has been in action behind the scenes the whole time to get to you what you need. He gives seed for bread, which is the staff of life. Bread speaks of your needs. He gives seed to meet the need. But His goal is not merely to meet your need. His goal, His desire, is not merely sufficiency. His goal for your life is *abundance.* So He says to you, "OK, if you will just sow the seed, I'll make sure the seed brings forth a harvest." He grants you seed and you are to take that seed and do two things with it: eat some and you redistribute the rest.

This is a process that Mammon does not want us to understand, follow, or even agree with. Mammon wants us to sow strictly into our own lives, into our own pockets. Mammon prefers that we hoard, because he knows the law of the sower—a principle he wants turned against us.

The Law of the Sower

The seeds that we sow always operate under three spiritual principles that comprise the Law of the Sower:

1. You only reap *what you sow.*

2. You only reap *after you sow.*

3. You always reap *more than you sow.*

Let's go back to Second Corinthians 9:10. It says that the God who supplies seed to the sower and bread for food will also *"supply and multiply the seed you have sown."* Notice that the seed you have already sown is going to be multiplied. A quick study of the terminology used by Paul tells us more about how this works.

The first time Paul uses the word *seed* in this verse it is the Greek word *sperma,*[5] from which we get the English word *sperm.* This seed has life in it. However, the seed that God multiplies is not the *sperma* seed, it's *sporran* seed. In other words, this seed that has a life force in it is *the seed that we have sown,* not the seed we eat.

God says that He multiplies *the seed sown;* He does not multiply the seed that you *keep,* the seed that you eat for yourself. The only seed that is multiplied is the seed that has been used for the needs of others. He doesn't even multiply the seed that you store in the bank, because once you bank it, it's in the world's system!

As we have learned, the world operates through buying and selling, but God's Kingdom operates through giving and receiving. In the world, you get addition from interest. In the Kingdom, God does not merely add interest, he *multiplies.* But here's the catch: He only multiplies what you sow. Thus, as Paul indicated in Galatians 6:7, if you sow little, you get little; if you sow much, you get much; if you sow nothing, you get nothing.

God says He's giving you seed for your need—but He does not stop there. He continues to pour. He takes you into abundance. *Your blessing is a multiplication of that which you sow.* Therefore, since you determine how much you sow, you are actually determining how much, or what, your harvest will be.

So what do you do with the extra? How do you handle the abundance God gives you? After you've taken care of your needs and your obligations—your rent or mortgage payment, your food and gas and utility bills and other expenses such as taking care of your grandmother or another family member who is in a retirement home—where does the rest of your money go? If you are sowing seed, then God will bless you with sufficiency to fulfill your obligations.

How to Handle the Overflow

We know that God will adhere to the text as He has revealed it to us. This means that He will take you beyond sufficiency and into abundance. But the greatest existential decision that you must make in your life is *how you will handle the overflow.* This is important, because overflow is where Mammon steps in and influences us to move out of need and into *greed.*

The answer we seek begins in the Book of Psalm:

> *Where is the man who fears the Lord? God will teach him to choose the best.*
> *He shall live within God's circle of blessing...* (Psalm 25:12-13 TLB).

There is a "circle of blessing" within which God desires me to live. Within that circle is found every need and every obligation I have. As God pours and releases favor, grace, mercy, provision, seed, and other blessings into my life, He fills up that circle.

Picture the circle as the top of a bucket. As God pours and releases blessings and favor and resources and seed into that bucket, there comes a point at which the needs within that circle are met. But *God keeps on pouring!* And as He pours, I move into the realm of overflow.

Remember that the question is this: "What do I do with the extra?" God says it is the Kingdom that is blessed by your overflow. That could mean somebody gets blessed whose cup is not as big as yours. Maybe it's someone whose circle is not as large as yours, or someone whose harvest was not as big as yours.

When God says, "I bless you," His next statement will be, "Now I want to use you to bless somebody else." God did not bless you just to give you a new car and a bigger house and a bigger bank account. He blessed you to have your needs met and to enable you to reach your desires—but also He wants you to turn around and bless somebody else. Your cup cannot truly "runneth over" (see Ps. 23:5 KJV) until it overflows to others!

The problem in society today, where Mammon runs rampant, is that most people consume the overflow on themselves. They "get" and they keep it all for their own needs and desires and little else.

> *"Get Place and Wealth, if possible with grace;*
> *If not, by any means get Wealth and Place."*
> —Alexander Pope; *Imitations of Horace*

There is a contemporary theology of prosperity that has so poisoned the spirit of most of the Church that we have become narcissistic, selfish, and stingy toward anything outside of ourselves. It's all about "getting" (often by any means). We have come to believe that the only reason God blesses us is for us. This extremist theology of prosperity has infected the Church with tunnel vision and has distorted our very relationship with God. We look to Him as someone whose only role is to give to us; we fail to regard passing on to others what He has given on to us. That which appears to be a pious and spiritual relationship with God has actually morphed into a spiritual manipulation of God, where even Christians are trying to *get, get, get* from Him.

This is why God's measurement is not about the size of your bank account or the size of your paycheck or the amount in your offering envelope; it's about the size of your heart. If you have a heart for the Kingdom, then you cannot help but have a desire and a concern for people outside of yourself.

Here again comes the question: *how much is enough?* With the kind of theology that has crept into the Body of Christ today, that question is rarely asked. How much is enough? Remember that, in order to get into abundance you must exceed a fixed position and a fixed measurement. *You will never be in abundance until you first define how much is enough to provide for your "fixed" needs.* Jesus Christ died owning nothing of material worth but His tunic. Mother Theresa died owning nothing but her sari. Dr. Bill Bright (my mentor from afar and a well-known man who determined not to accumulate wealth in his last decade of life) died owning nothing.

And there are those who, out of the great financial abundance God poured into their lives (such as Bill Bright, Billy Graham, and countless others), chose to reflow that abundance out of their lives and into the work of God's Kingdom.

I'm getting to the specific principle I want to share with you and I warn you that, if you miss it, you will mistakenly admire Mother Theresa and Bill Bright (who died with nothing), far more than you will admire those who give away millions of dollars to God's work.

Many people give to God's Kingdom; some give out of God's *overflow*. Imagine what is in the cup of those who are presently able to give away millions of dollars without putting a dent in their finances. Imagine if they resist the enticement of the spirit of the world, ignore the influence of Mammon, and *give*—to the poor, the disenfranchised, the powerless, and the needy.

Do not get caught up in a poverty mentality—that spirit of "holy poverty" that makes people think they're more spiritual if they're more broke. Yet, consider this: I believe that if the 2 percent of the wealthiest Americans who own or control 95 percent of the wealth in the United States would let some of that vast wealth flow out to the truly needy, poverty would be eliminated in this country.

God speaks to our hearts. There's a calling that He has on your life. For some, His calling is to make do on more meager income and to give of *yourself* as abundance into the lives of others. For others, His call is to have resources and the ability to sow material, monetary resources into the Kingdom, to "sponsor the show" and pay for the troupe to do what they do for the people.

I believe the Lord has called some to be very wealthy and rich (by our common understanding of the word *rich*). However, I also believe those that He has called to be rich have been called to be vessels of blessings to others on a much higher financial level than they currently are.

While it is Mammon who perpetuates a poverty mentality, Mammon is also the one who creates a greed mentality. Is your life driven by seed, by need, or by greed? To have a heart that beats like the heart of Christ, is to have a heart after God's own heart. He will take you from the place where you strive to have your own needs met, to the place where you are looking for someone whose needs you can meet.

Some people, for example, are blessed to be able to put a child through college. Others struggle to put themselves through college. But wouldn't it be great to use some of the blessings God has poured into our lives to provide a scholarship for a needy child who otherwise wouldn't be able to go? Now that you have provided your son or daughter with higher education, it may be that God wants you to help provide for somebody else's child. It may be that God is trying to put you in a position where you can look for ways to bless others. Maybe God is trying to get you to a place where you're able to write the check and sow into a ministry that advances the Gospel.

Maybe He wants you to get three or four or five other families together to pool financial resources and "adopt" a homeless or struggling family. He may be waiting on your group to help them get into an apartment and buy a car so they can get to work each day. You might be the ones He's calling to buy them some gas or car insurance or warm jackets or clothing or groceries until they get a leg up.

If we pool our resources, we can pick up more of the financial slack for those who are struggling to make ends meet. There are plenty of ways to spread our overflow to God's children in need, and there are plenty of people in need in every community. As Jesus said in John 12:8, Mark 14:7, and Matthew 26:11, we will always have the poor among us (which seems to indicate that Mammon is doing a good job keeping people in a gathering and hoarding mentality rather than a sharing and giving one). But it also means there will always be opportunities to bless those who are less fortunate than you are.

I want to live in God's overflow. I want to live where the abundance that God gives me is at His disposal. I want to be able to get out there and provide help to people who are less fortunate. Many people know the pain and the frustration of being in a church worship service or being in a situation when God speaks to their heart to give or to sow or to help someone with a monetary need, but when they open the checkbook, the money is gone. God reminds them of the $200 spent the week before on something that they really didn't need and could easily have done without. Had that $200 been available now, the answer to God's request would have been "Yes!"

It's not just the large impulse purchases that hamstring our finances. Imagine what four or five months' worth of gourmet coffee beverages adds up to! It could easily mean $200 of savings that could help someone who is struggling—a person for whom $20 is a huge amount and $200 means having a roof over their head.

Peter had boats. He was a fisherman. One day Jesus asked him for one of his boats to preach on (see Luke 5:3). Jesus had need of it. On another occasion, as Jesus was preparing to enter Jerusalem for the last time, He instructed two disciples to go into town, untie a donkey, and tell the bystanders that the Lord needed it (see Mark 11:2-3).

I want to be so far into the overflow that when God says, "I have need of your resources to bless that person over there," I am able to bless them without hesitation. I want to be able to write the check. I want to be able to provide for the need. I want to be the lender and not the borrower. I want to be able to sponsor them. I want to be able to help them to be what God has called them to be. I want to live in the overflow and set an example of what God can do with a willing heart and an obedient spirit.

I don't want to be caught short because I spent needlessly on myself. I'm not saying that you should keep yourself poor. I'm encouraging you to use God's resources, His blessings, and His abundance, wisely, with His heart and for His purposes. God does not mind your *having stuff*, He only asks that you *share* with those in need.

God wants to bless you so much that you would be in a position to bless even those who didn't want to see you prosper. What a testimony that would be for God and against the spirit of Mammon. I want to live in the overflow for the sake of the Kingdom. I want to draw closer to God. I want to live my life in His presence.

He gives you seed and He gives you bread, and then He multiplies your seed, so you can give more—and that triggers His giving you more still, because He knows He can trust you with it. He knows that you will share those greater riches with people in need. That's God's circle of blessing.

What an exciting circle to be in!

Endnotes

1. *Biblesoft's New Exhaustive Strong's Numbers and Concordance with Expanded Greek-Hebrew Dictionary.* CD-ROM. Biblesoft, Inc. and International Bible Translators, Inc. s.v. "dunateo," (NT 1414).

2. Ibid., "dunamia" (NT 1410).

3. Ibid., "eulogia," (NT 2129) and "eulogeo" (NT 2127).

4. *Strong's Dictionary,* "epichoregeo" (G2023), *to fully supply.*

5. *Strong's Dictionary,* "sperma" (G4690), seed, offspring, remnant.

Notes

Chapter Ten

CLOSING THE CIRCLE

Where is the man who fears the Lord? God will teach him how to choose the best. He shall live within God's circle of blessing, and his children shall inherit the earth (Psalm 25:12-13 TLB).

SOME of what I write here amounts to a difficult word—but I write it with as much love as I can muster. I want God to prepare us, or more accurately, to set us in the position where our minds and eyes and ears are open for this very challenging word.

There has been a secret oppression with which many people have been dealing. It is a secret struggle of which most are rather ashamed. I believe in my spirit that, for some of us, the tithe offering has become a difficult blessing to partake of. This is a challenging time for many—not because of what's in our hearts, but because of the situation regarding our financial ability or lack thereof. I don't believe for a moment that those of you who are not giving regularly are withholding because of a hard heart. What I do believe is that there is an oppression, an attack of the enemy in general, and of Mammon in particular. Many who truly love the Lord are experiencing the oppressive grip of the spirit of Mammon upon their lives.

Psalms 25:12 in the New King James Version says, *"Who is the man that fears the Lord? Him shall He teach in the way He chooses."* The Living Bible paraphrases that verse this way: *"Where is the man who fears the Lord? God will teach him how to choose the best."* The Living Bible goes on to say, *"He shall live within God's circle of blessing. . ."* (Ps. 25:13).

As we learned in the previous chapter, the goal of our lives is to live within God's circle of blessing. The one who fears, worships, prioritizes, is committed to, loves, and esteems the Lord is the one who shall live within God's circle of blessing. Close the circle and you are protected.

Abundance

As we learned in a previous chapter, apostle Paul said the following in Second Corinthians 9:6-8:

> *Remember this—if you give little, you will get little. A farmer who plants just a few seeds will get only a small crop, but if he plants much, he will reap much. Everyone must make up his own mind as to how much he should give. Don't force anyone to give more than he really wants to, for cheerful givers are the ones God prizes. God is able to make it up to you by giving you everything you need and more so that there will not only be enough for your own needs but plenty left over to give joyfully to others* (TLB).

God is the one who grants grace, and it is the grace to *give*. The context is about giving; giving is a "grace gift" of God. It is called, in the Greek, a *charis*[1], from which we get the words *charisma* and *charismatic*. Just as we should have an "attitude of gratitude" when receiving, we also need to have a graciousness of giving: "not grudgingly or of necessity; for God loves a cheerful giver" (see 2 Cor. 9:7).

Everything God does is for a specific purpose. Watch the flow as described in the passage: God gives everything we need. He gives so that we might have sufficiency—but He does not stop there. He has a higher purpose. His goal is for us to have plenty left over. He gives us the grace we need to have a sufficient amount *and* to move past sufficiency to the place where we have an abundance to give joyfully to others.

You'll remember that *sufficiency* involves having enough, while *abundance* means having more than enough. Thus, God's goal is for you to live in a condition of "abounding abundance."

Back to Psalms 25:12-13: We are to live in the circle of God's blessing. What is in this circle of blessing? It is *abundance that flows through your life.* Sufficiency is the need-meeting provision that flows *into* your life. Abundance is the overflow that passes *out of* your life and into the lives of others.

What, then, constitutes the closed circle, God's basic provision for you before the overflow begins? Three things: your obligations (what you must do), your wants (with a caveat: you don't always get what you want), and your needs (what you must have). Let's examine how not dealing with these three areas can prevent us from closing the circle and thereby stop any overflow from coming our way.

I. Our Obligations

This area contains the greatest trap of the enemy Mammon. Our obligations are a commentary on our debt—the monetary commitments we have made. Most people never get to the overflow because they are stuck meeting their debts and obligations.

> You have sown much, and bring in little; you eat, but do not have enough; you drink, but you are not filled with drink; you clothe yourselves, but no one is warm; and he who earns wages, earns wages to put into a bag with holes (Haggai 1:6).

The will of God is that money would become your *slave;* not that you would become a slave to the money you owe. You know you are a slave to debt when your working helps to make someone else rich. As we have learned, money is a tool designed to facilitate Kingdom causes. It is a means by which God blesses His people, and it is a means through which God's people bless the Kingdom. Yet, many Christians have made themselves slaves to debt. It is the cagey devil Mammon who has convinced the world that debt is fine. "No problem!" he says. "Debt is normal—*necessary*, even!"

When you live your life simply paying and paying and paying off debts, when you have no alternative but to be in debt, when you never seem to have enough money to do what you want to do, when you work hard and have nothing to show for it, you may be in bondage to debt. It's not that you don't have the desire to give, it's that when it's time to give, you are unable to do so.

If this applies to you, begin by binding the spirit of guilt that people have or will put on you for never quite having enough. At the same time, be real enough to recognize that you are not yet where God wants you to be.

The problem is not just being in debt. The greater problem is that the situation can deteriorate until you are so far in debt *that you can't pay back the obligation*. This is how the enemy attacks us. The devil is not so much impressed by how much you shout and praise the Lord, especially not when you're shouting and praising while you're in debt and bondage and broke with no means to pay and no plan to try. The devil makes a mockery of that when he accuses you before God.

Please do not misunderstand me. This is not a wealth and prosperity position—that is neither my point nor my teaching. I am only trying to explain that if you have the desire to sow, but you don't have the resources to sow, it is difficult to see how you could ever get involved in the Second Corinthians 9 process of sowing and reaping. God's will is to give you enough to accomplish your heart's desire *and* bless others. His will is for you to be actively blessing the Kingdom and causing souls to be won for Christ.

Psalms 37:21 says, *"The wicked borrows and does not repay...."* The Bible says that those who have debts and fail to pay are wicked. The phrase "does not repay" is not speaking so much of their character as of their condition. The revelation of the text involves a person who is not paying their debt. It's not so much that they don't want to pay; it is more likely that they can't pay. It implies that they can't pay because they're so far in debt. They are so over-extended that they can't make good on their obligations.

Wicked is one of several synonyms for "sin." It is a sin to not pay your bills. But if Mammon is the one enticing us to get into debt in the first place, then why is it a sin not to repay? It is sin because somewhere down the line you made a vow, a pledge, a promise. You accepted money or merchandise from somebody and you gave your word that you were going to repay them. Your word was on the line, not Mammon's. When you dishonor your word, you have, in effect, lied retroactively.

Now let's look at the remaining portion of Psalms 37:21: *"But the righteous shows mercy and gives."* "They show mercy" means that they sow; they are being a blessing to someone else. The emphasis of the text is found in the juxtaposition of the two phrases: on the one side is a person who is behaving wickedly because they made a promise and did not carry it through; on the other side is a person who is righteous because they give. The picture is a comparison between a person who is acting sinfully and a person who is in right standing with God.

Therefore, what is one way to tell if a person is wicked? They make vows (have entered into debts) that they cannot pay. How do you know a person is righteous? Because they are able to bless others and give.

There are those who have drifted into sin. Not so much willingly or because they are evil people, but because circumstantially they have evolved into a condition where they cannot meet their obligations. In short, they have allowed themselves to become entrapped in a devil's snare.

2. Our Wants

The Lord God said to the woman, "What is this you have done?" The woman said, "The serpent deceived me, and I ate" (Genesis 3:13).

It is not a sin to want. The key is in *what* we want and how far we're willing to go to get it. Often our wants are legitimate, such as the desire to do a favor for someone who has been kind or helpful or generous to us. It is legitimate to want a better, more solid, safer car, or a larger home in which to more comfortably fit a growing family. At other times, however, our wants can get us into trouble.

The best example of acting on inappropriate wants occurred in The Garden of Eden. It began with a cleverly crafted deception in Genesis 3:1. Here, the serpent (the devil) manipulated Eve; he deceived her. When you *deceive* someone, you are leading them astray, beguiling them, seducing them.

There is no indication in this account of Eve and the tree of the knowledge of good and evil that Eve had ever expressed interest in the fruit of the tree. It's as though the devil took opportunity; he saw her heading in the general direction of the tree and so he slithered into its branches.

Then, as Eve passed by, he called out to her. "Psst! *Psst*—hey, Eve. Up here. In the tree. C'mere, baby." He may very well have been munching on the forbidden fruit himself. Then he lowered the bait: "Did God *really* tell you guys, 'You shall not eat of every tree of The Garden'?"

> *And the woman said to the serpent, "We may eat the fruit of the trees of the garden; but of the fruit of the tree which is in the midst of the garden, God has said, 'You shall not eat it, nor shall you touch it, lest you die.'" Then the serpent said to the woman, "You will not surely die. For God knows that in the day you eat of it your eyes will be opened, and you will be like God, knowing good and evil." So when the woman saw that the tree was good for food, that it was pleasant to the eyes, and a tree desirable to make one wise, she took of its fruit and ate...* (Genesis 3:2-6).

Eve confirmed that God had told Adam not to eat its fruit. She then added the part about not touching the tree. The trouble is that she engaged in a discussion with the cleverest of beasts, and he went to work on her like a chef carving a ham. First he insinuated that the fruit must be pretty darn great, since it belonged to God. He dropped the bait even lower by "wondering" aloud why in the world God would want to keep something so wonderful for Himself.

Then the serpent explained to Eve that she surely must have misunderstood what God said. Perhaps her eyes darted toward the fruit as the devil drew her into his web. The clincher was a three-pronged pinscher attack: He convinced her that the fruit was only food (*"the woman saw that the tree was good for food"*). He made her aware that it looked inviting (*"it was pleasant to the eyes"*). Then he closed the deal with something Adam and Eve probably had no understanding of at the time (but were about to learn the hard way)—he told them the fruit would make them wise (*"a tree desirable to make one wise"*). That was the final blow.

Satan tempted Eve to take something she may very well have had no interest in taking. Even if she'd had a passing curiosity about it, she didn't take the fruit until the devil got her attention, enticed her, and beguiled her. She was distracted by the devil's discussion of the object. She considered it. She decided that she wanted it. She took it. She was tricked because she was tempted. She yielded and took what she wanted *but did not need*—and was, in fact, told by God to avoid completely.

God had told Adam and Eve that they had all they needed in The Garden. He told them all was theirs except that one tree. The trick satan used was simple: "You need more. You're entitled to more. Why should God keep you from having more? Surely you want *this.*" The trap was set. And right up to the instant she plucked that forbidden fruit from the branch, Eve could have chosen not to take it. She took it simply because *she wanted it.*

It's not always as clear as it was in Eve's case that a certain want or desire is against God's Word. What is clear is that our wants can work against us when we don't carefully consider the consequences before we act on our desire and take what we want.

3. Our Needs

What are you paying for that you didn't need? How does the enemy customize your temptations? How does the enemy present it in your favorite shade and your perfect size? How does he put something before you that tempts, tantalizes, and tricks you into taking on something that would attract only you?

He messes with your ego. You indulge the desire for what you think you lack. You end up buying something you don't need, with money you don't have, to impress people you don't even know. Then you say, "I can't wear *that* outfit. I wore it last week" (as if the hundreds of people you passed by that week took note of what you were wearing—as though they even cared what you were wearing).

Here again, it is not a sin to have needs. We all have needs. We need to put a roof over our heads, so we have to pay rent or a mortgage. We need to keep fed, so we have to buy food. We need to stay warm, so we must purchase clothing, and so on. The key is in how we define *need* versus how the spirit of Mammon wants us to define *need*.

The Psalms 25:12-13 passage about the "circle of blessing" paints a picture of a person who has learned how to do things God's way. By contrast, Psalms 37:21 describes the "wicked"—someone who is so far in debt that they cannot repay.

How does such a predicament begin? It happens because you are deceived. You are deceived into thinking that you need what you don't need. You are paying credit card bills for things you can't even wear anymore or that have gone out of fashion. We fall into these traps because we are deceived by a master manipulator, one whose sole…full-time…daily purpose is to get us off track and *keep us off.*

The Bible says that our treasure will be where our heart is (see Matt. 6:21; Luke 12:34). It also says that, as we think in our hearts, so we are (see Prov. 23:7). The enemy tricks us because he plays on our fragile egos—our need to be liked, our need to impress, our need to be seen, our need to be affirmed and recognized. So we spend all of our "stuff" as though we were putting it in pockets with holes in them (see Hag. 1:6) because *the ego never has enough.*

The fashion industry is a billion-dollar industry because it tells people who don't have the flashiest wardrobe that they need it. I'm not saying that you should run around looking shabby. Not at all. It's OK; in fact, it's good to look sharp. But the question of abundance is never answered until we tackle the question: *How much is enough?*

You can never get into abundance until you exceed this fixed point of measurement. If the equation is: $y = abundance$, I can never solve for the value of y until I define the baseline of how much is enough. The value of "enough" is the measuring point of my need; it is the level of provision that is just below the place of abundance. If I need $10 but I only have $3, I am nowhere near approaching abundance. If I need $10 and have $12, I am in abundance, because I have exceeded what I need.

God's goal for our lives is that we live in abundance. The prophet Habakkuk said, *"The just shall live by his faith"* (Hab. 2:4). But what many people call *faith* is actually *presumption*; and what others call faith is merely foolishness. Against such as these, the prophet said:

> Will not all these take up a proverb against him, and a taunting riddle against him, and say, "Woe to him who increases what is not his—how long? And to him who loads himself with many pledges"? Will not your creditors rise up suddenly? Will they not awaken who oppress you? And you will become their booty (Habakkuk 2:6-7).

Booty is the prize, the spoils, the plunder of war. If you don't have enough money to pay your bills, your creditors will go after you and make your life miserable until you settle up with them. You'll be in bondage to them until you pay them back. I've been there. There was a time in my life when I couldn't buy a pencil.

Follow the Money

In the movie *All the President's Men*, Deep Throat was coaching Woodward and Bernstein as to how to solve the suspected criminal activities emanating from the White House. The instruction Deep Throat gave the reporters over and over again was frightfully simple: "Follow the money."

Track the money. You'll never get into God's overflow of blessings until you understand what's coming in and where it is going. We need to get really practical. Our deliverance from the demon of debt, from the enticements of Mammon, from the devil's snare, will take more than just prayer. It's not a problem of what you make. Prosperity and abundance are rarely—if ever—about the amount of your monetary income. Wealth and prosperity are never defined by the size of your bank account.

It cannot be repeated enough: God's will is that you live in abundance, which is beyond sufficiency. Sufficiency assumes that your bills and obligations are being met. Many people spend up to two-thirds of their take-home income servicing debts. Interest. Credit cards. Car loans. Some people don't even understand that they can get to the point where they own their home—not just the 5 or 10 or 15 percent they put down on the mortgage. They don't realize that the ideal is to *own the home outright and mortgage-free!* For them, it's an entirely new level of thinking. It's a mind shift.

The point is that we must first get a handle on our debts and obligations and on our needs and wants. Some of us need to make a burnt offering: Burn the credit cards. We need to sacrifice those cards on the altar. Too many are bound to those cards as surely as a slave has shackles on his hands and feet. They are as much in bondage as any slave.

Here's an assignment: For the next 60 days, *follow the money*. Rather than putting your money in a pocket with holes and watching it vanish into thin air, track your money—figure out what you spend it on. You will never get deliverance from Mammon until you learn how to manage your money, and you will never learn how to manage your money until you learn where it is and where it's going.

Do you want to start putting Mammon under your feet? Start by getting a pulse on your spending habits. Once you see where your money is going, you'll know where your heart is. And once you identify your motives, you can reestablish and redirect your priorities to break the grip of financial struggle—and never again be trapped by a devil's snare.

Endnote

1. *Strong's Dictionary*, "charis" (G5485), graciousness of manner, divine influence upon the heart, gratitude.

Notes

Chapter Eleven

MAMMON AND GOD'S TITHE

As we have learned throughout this book, the world's system operates on buying and selling, while the Kingdom of God operates on giving and receiving. The world's system (which is controlled by the fallen angel Jesus referred to as "Mammon") operates on the principle that there is a finite supply, or scarcity, of goods.

Therefore, it follows that the goods must be controlled (and indeed are controlled by a certain few). It also follows that, because there is a scarcity, the world is divided into two often sharply contrasting groups: the "haves" and the "have nots."

In brief, the guiding principle of the man-made monetary system is that *there's only so much to go around.* The principle of God's Kingdom is that *there's an abundance.*

The Bible says that God is able to release favor and grace so that you might abound, that there might be abundance (see 2 Cor. 9:8). There are many translations of this verse, but they all agree with each another:

The New International Version of the Bible says that God is willing to release grace upon you *so that you will have all you need.*

The New King James Version says, *that you might have an abundance.*

The Living Bible says, *that you might have enough for your needs and plenty left over.*

The Amplified Bible says, that you will possess *"enough to require no aid or support and furnished in abundance for every good work and charitable donation...."*

Each of these versions and translations points to one clear truth: God's goal is to bless you so that you might be a blessing to someone else. His desire is that the blessings that flow to you might flow through you as a *channel* (as opposed to a receptacle) of blessing to others.

Seed: What It Does

In Chapter 9, we discussed what seed is and how God operates "behind the scenes" to bring forth a crop from the seed we sow. I'm not going to do an in-depth study of tithing here (for that, you can read the chapter on tithing in my book *Making Your Money Count*). For now, know this: The spirit of Mammon attacks our tithe; he does all he can to corrupt our understanding of this key principle of sowing and reaping. Therefore, I want us to briefly examine the operation of seed in the context of the tithe:

> *He who supplies seed to the sower and bread for food will also supply and increase your store of seed and will enlarge the harvest of your righteousness* (2 Corinthians 9:10 NIV).

As we have learned, in the context of this verse, *He* is God. He releases and gives seed for those who will sow it. The word *seed* is a metaphor for several things, including male children (that which is produced from male seed or sperm), and the Word of God, as described in the parable of the sower (see Matt. 13:18-23).

In the context of Second Corinthians 9, the word *seed* refers to that which we give. (Second Corinthians 9:7 says that *"God loves a cheerful giver."*) We have also learned that if we sow sparingly, we will reap sparingly; and if we sow bountifully, we will reap bountifully (see 2 Cor. 9:6).

Therefore, the context of *seed* is that which God gives to us within the economy of the culture. It is whatever constitutes the medium of exchange in a given society. In the days of Paul, seed was spoken of in an agrarian or agricultural context. Bartering, trade, and sales were based on harvest that grew out of seed.

The first purpose for which God gives us resources (money, riches, finances, and material possessions) is for sowing. It is no accident that in describing God in the Second Corinthians 9 passage, Paul called Him, *"He who supplies seed to the sower."* Sowing is listed first in this series of reasons that God gave for our having money and resources. This is because sowing speaks of *the tithe* as a seed for sowing, for depositing, into the storehouse: tithe as seed; storehouse as soil.

The key to sowing is not only about the seed itself, but also about the "soil" into which the seed is planted and the *kind* of "soil" that the seed is planted into (see Matt. 13:4-8 and Mark 4:3-8). Even the best seed yields no crop if it is deposited in bad soil. In this context, the passage is obviously referring to *giving*. Etymologically, the literal meaning of the word *tithe* has to do with "the tenth part."[1] The Bible says that the seed/tithe is to be brought in and deposited into the soil/ storehouse of God's Kingdom:

> *"Bring the whole tithe into the storehouse, that there may be food in My house. Test Me in this,"* says the Lord Almighty, *"and see if I will not throw open the floodgates of heaven and pour out so much blessing that you will not have room enough for it"* (Malachi 3:10 NIV).

As the text indicates, the tithe is a commandment from God, the adherence to which brings a promise from God: "Do this and I'll bless you so much you won't be able to keep track of it."[2]

The tithe is not the answer to all of your financial problems. If you are tithing off your income and you are still spending more than you earn, tithing won't help you with that. The tithe is not a quick-fix to clean up your credit rating. The tithe will not solve your financial problems. If you start tithing today but you don't pay your bills, you will still have debt collectors after you.

Sometimes tithing is taught with the idea that once you start tithing, your financial situation is going to suddenly blossom. Tithing is not the solution to all of your financial problems! You don't get into right standing with God just by doing a work or an act. You don't work your way up to grace. The judgment of God is removed from you by your repentance, by your turning away from previous practices that were against the Word of God, and by coming into right standing with Him, thus creating a circumstance where God's favor can be released unto your life.

The Bible says, *"Bring the whole tithe into the storehouse"* (Mal. 3:10 NIV). What is the storehouse for? It's where food, meat, provisions, are stored. Nehemiah 12:44 says the storehouse in Nehemiah's time was for *"the offerings, the firstfruits, and the tithes."* The storehouse for us in our modern society, the "soil" into which we sow our tithe, is the place where we are fed spiritually. Some churchgoers are eating all over town, going to this church and that church. But for most of us, the tithe is to be planted where we are spiritually nurtured, where we are growing in the Word, studying the Word, being challenged by the Word—where the Spirit of God is empowering His Word in our lives, and where we are being changed by it.

The place where you receive spiritual "meat," is the place from which God's spiritual provisions are dispersed. We know this is the case because the paradigm, the picture, the metaphor, that is used in the biblical context of tithing is that of an agrarian society: when the harvest comes up, you bring forth the tenth part of the crop. Our harvest would be the income we produce, the wages we earn.

The tithe is not to be held back; it is to be released when you get it. Deuteronomy and Nehemiah talk about the tithe provisions, food and all those other things that are brought to the temple storehouse. These resources are dispersed to the priests and the gatekeepers and the musicians and Levites and strangers and orphans and widows. The tithe promotes ministry and provides for people—particularly those in need.[3]

To Build Faith

Tithing increases our faith. Strong faith is key to ignoring the manipulations, enticements, and trickery of Mammon. Tithing binds our heart and trust to God.

Many people don't tithe because they fear that if they give God one tenth of the money He gave them, they will run short somewhere else. God is only asking for 10 percent, yet they are afraid they can't make it on 90 percent of what He gives them! First John 4:18 tells us that God's perfect love casts out fear. Second

Timothy 1:7 says that God has not given us a spirit of fear. So what is the source of the fear of not being able to make ends meet on 90 percent of what we bring home?

The spirit of Mammon wants to convince you that you don't need to tithe or that you cannot afford to pay the tithe. The reality is this: If you are on such a financial precipice that you can't live on 90 percent of your income, then you may need to consider downsizing your lifestyle by at least 10 percent.

Tithing promotes faith and removes fear. This kind of financial fear is a *spirit of fear* controlled by the spirit, Mammon. This demon will tell you not to give God what is due Him because you'll miss what you think is due you. But if the Bible says that fear does not come from God, then a simple process of elimination tells you where fear does come from.

Who are you going to believe—your God, or your adversary? The only way to cast out fear concerning your provision is to trust God. *Trust* is not only a noun; it is also a verb. Don't just say it; *do it.* Trust Him. It promotes faith and protects us from the influence of Mammon. Faith causes you to see God doing with your finances what your calculator said could not be done. Trust God with 10 percent and see if He doesn't do more with the 90 percent that's left than you could have done with the whole thing.

The enemy says that if you tithe, you won't make it on the remaining 90 percent. The spirit of the living God says that, if you don't tithe, you can't make it on 100 percent of your income! God says, "Trust Me, because I'm going to open the windows of Heaven and pour you out such a blessing, you cannot contain it."

Tithing protects us from Mammon. Tithing proves God from Genesis through Revelation. And between all that Scripture, there's only one place where God dares us to *challenge* Him to trust him. One place!

> *"Bring the full tithe into the storehouse, so that there may be food in My house, and thus* **put Me to the test**," *says the Lord of hosts; "see if I will not open the windows of heaven for you and pour down for you an overflowing blessing"* (Malachi 3:10 NRSV).

It's About the Heart

It is possible to bring the tithe and *not* be a tither. The paradigm of giving is found in Genesis:

> *In the process of time it came to pass that Cain brought an offering of the fruit of the ground to the Lord. Abel also brought of the firstborn of his flock and of their fat. And the Lord respected Abel and his offering, but He did not respect Cain and his offering. And Cain was very angry, and his countenance fell. So the Lord said to Cain, "Why are you angry? And why has your countenance fallen? If you do well, will you not be accepted? And if you do not do well, sin lies at the door. And its desire is for you, but you should rule over it"* (Genesis 4:3-7).

Cain and Abel both brought an offering to God. The Bible says that Cain brought of the fruit of the ground. Abel brought of his flock, or livestock. Many times this text has been interpreted as saying that the reason Cain's offering was not accepted is because he brought of the fruit of the ground—a crop offering—whereas Abel brought a blood offering. I beg to differ, because there are times when God also affirms tithing in the medium of crops or harvest, so that could not have been the critical difference.

Remember, the tithe is given in the context of the medium of exchange of the culture and every culture has various mediums of exchange. The exchange of harvest or crops was as legitimate as the exchange of livestock. The difference in Cain's and Abel's offerings would be akin to the difference in their individual lines of work. They both brought an offering and they both brought it out of their particular income levels and professions—one as a farmer, the other as a rancher.

However, Abel brought of the first things of his flock *and* of the fat thereof. The fat was the most valuable part of the animal. Different parts of an animal have varying degrees of value. Some parts are more valuable than others. That Abel brought the first of the flock and the fat thereof, means this: *he went the extra mile* and carved out the most precious part of the animal. He could have just brought the plain old sacrificial animal, but he went beyond the minimum requirement.

Genesis 4:4 says that the Lord "respected," (or "looked with favor upon," or "accepted") Abel's offering. Yet, He did not receive the offering of Cain and Cain became very angry at God. The difference in the two men was not in the offering itself, but in the *attitude behind the offering.* I love what God says to Cain in verses six and seven. He scolds him, basically saying, "What's wrong with you, Cain? Why are you so upset, boy? If you would adjust your attitude and give with a less grudging spirit, your offering would be accepted, too."

The difference between one who brings the tithe and one who is a tither is *attitude*—how you respond in your heart to what you bring to God. The key is not so much in the substance of the offering as it is in the mind-set behind the offering. God is not just looking for the tenth, because the tenth is about *amount.* Cain and Abel both brought offerings, but they had different attitudes about them. The one who simply brings the tithe, brings the right amount with the wrong attitude. A tither not only brings the right amount; a true tither brings his or her heart.

What kind of attitude shift do you make when it's time for the offering in your church? Do you slip out the back door just before the offering is taken, or arrive just late enough to have missed the offering? How often does the call for the offering shift you out of your shout of joy? It's amazing how the Holy Ghost lifts us. I believe the day is coming when Christians will offer more than just a few cute little songs before they put 2 or 3 percent in the tithe plate.

I say this, because when you give your offering, God will push the flashback button on your life. He'll run the instant replay and bring to memory all that He has brought you through. How He has blessed you. How He has been faithful to you. How He has put food on your table when you didn't have the money. How He brought people into your life at just the right time with just the right gift when you needed it most.

Don't let Mammon quench your spirit when it's time to give. You know how good God has been to you. God Himself says that it's our attitude that makes our offerings acceptable.

It's *All* God's Anyway!

All the tithe of the land, whether of the seed of the land or of the fruit of the tree, is the Lord's. It is holy to the Lord (Leviticus 27:30).

How then do we handle our seed so that it is deposited, or laid up, for us in Heaven? First of all, we are to acknowledge that *it belongs to God.* Speak to yourself and say, "Self, this is not mine; it's God's."

Stewardship is all about how you manage and handle and control that which someone else owns. He is watching with a keen eye how you handle what He has given you. We don't give God the tithe, *we return it back to Him!* The first thing you must understand is that the tenth part brings with it a fiduciary responsibility; it is your part to *handle it in a way that honors God.* Equally important is that *it is holy unto the Lord. Holy* means that it is set apart, set aside for His use and His use only—He alone determines how it will serve the Kingdom.

An example of how keeping the tithe holy unto God relates to our handling of money, riches, finances, and material possessions, would be the process of buying a house. When you buy real estate, there is an escrow account into which you put a certain amount of money. That money can only be used for that house. It is consecrated, dedicated to one purpose. Period.

You must declare that money as being set aside, because it is now off limits to you. It does not matter if your child needs college tuition, or you need a new suit. It does not matter if your wife needs her hair done, or anything else needs done; you cannot take one cent of that escrow money. You can no longer handle it as though it's your money.

Once it's in the escrow account, the money is set aside for that house. If you somehow manage to get into the account and take a little something out of it—if you go to the showroom and buy a new set of wheels—then you have taken money that was set aside for one purpose and used it for another purpose (your own personal benefit). You might even face criminal or civil charges, because that money was contractually set aside.

The tithe, then, is a kind of escrow account held by God for credit to your "treasures in Heaven account." When you fail to treat it as holy, then you have taken that which belongs to God and have used it for your own personal benefit.

The key with the earthly escrow account is that the money set aside is there for a reason. When the deal closes you get a blessing: your new house. Neither you nor your spouse wants to mess with that. It's the same with God: He says that when we take what belongs to Him and desecrate it for our own wants, we are in danger of having *nothing* deposited into our account with Him in Heaven. In other words, we risk missing out on blessings for ourselves and quite possibly for our entire family, just because of our malfeasance.

A great example of this occurred in Joshua's day, when God had declared that the first city Israel would face when they went into Canaan would be Jericho. Jericho was to be *cherem*, devoted, to God as a sort of first-fruit sacrifice:

> *Now the city shall be doomed by the Lord to destruction, it and all who are in it. Only Rahab the harlot shall live, she and all who are with her in the house, because she hid the messengers that we sent. And you, by all means abstain from the accursed things, lest you become accursed when you take of the accursed things, and make the camp of Israel a curse, and trouble it. But all the silver and gold, and vessels of bronze and iron, are consecrated to the LORD; they shall come into the treasury of the LORD* (Joshua 6:17-19).

But somebody got a little greedy and ignored God's command:

> *But the children of Israel committed a trespass regarding the accursed things, for Achan the son of Carmi, the son of Zabdi, the son of Zerah, of the tribe of Judah, took of the accursed things; so the anger of the Lord burned against the children of Israel* (Joshua 7:1).

Achan didn't do what God told them to do. God had instructed them that everything was to be destroyed. But Achan took some of the spoils and hid them among his own property. The result was that the very next town they were to take, a little village called Ai, which had but a few people in it, routed Joshua's army:

So about three thousand men went up there from the people, but they fled before the men of Ai. And the men of Ai struck down about thirty-six men, for they chased them from before the gate as far as Shebarim, and struck them down on the descent; therefore the hearts of the people melted and became like water (Joshua 7:4-5).

The result of Achan's disobedience was that the nation lost a battle against a much smaller army, all because one man kept riches they had been instructed not to keep. God said:

Israel has sinned, and they have also transgressed My covenant which I commanded them. For they have even taken some of the accursed things, and have both stolen and deceived; and they have also put it among their own stuff. Therefore the children of Israel could not stand before their enemies, but turned their backs before their enemies, because they have become doomed to destruction. . . (Joshua 7:11-12).

When you desecrate that which belongs to God, you make yourself vulnerable to the attack of the enemy, because you have co-mingled things that were to be consecrated to God and have mingled them with your things.

God is telling us: "Let there be an attitude check: Bring the tithe into My storehouse and try Me. See if I won't open the windows of Heaven and pour you out a blessing." Every time I test God on this and tithe, it gives God an opportunity to prove Himself to me. It gives God a chance to make a liar out of the spirit of Mammon. It builds my faith in God. It banishes my fears about money, riches, finances, and material possessions.

That's the promise that is connected with the tithe. Don't ever let the fallen angel named Mammon steal your tithe—after all, it is *God* whom Mammon would be helping you to rob:

Will a man rob God? Yet you have robbed Me! But you say, "In what way have we robbed You?" In tithes and offerings (Malachi 3:8).

Endnotes

1. *Biblesoft's New Exhaustive Strong's Numbers and Concordance with Expanded Greek-Hebrew Dictionary.* CD-ROM. Biblesoft, Inc. and International Bible Translators, Inc. s.v. "ma'aser" (OT 4643) and "dekatos" (NT 1183).

2. Some suggest that the tithe is an Old Testament principle. Leviticus 27:30 says, *"All the tithe of the land, whether of the seed of the land or of the fruit of the tree, is the Lord's. It is holy to the LORD."* I won't yield to the temptation to chase a theological rabbit on this point, but there are many teachings that argue the validity of the tithe as a viable contemporary principle. I deal with this topic in my book *Making Your Money Count*, but suffice it to say, I am hard pressed to find anywhere in the Bible where it says something even remotely akin to, "The tithe is no longer the Lord's and it is no longer Holy."

3. Nowhere in Scripture is it stated that the tithe was to be used to build or purchase a building. The tithe was not used to build the tabernacle and the temple. The money for the construction of God's "house" was provided through offerings, which are donations over and above the tithe.

Notes

Conclusion

ABOVE ALL ELSE

GOD doesn't want our money, He wants our hearts. Giving your heart to Him starts with an attitude check and a reality check. Nothing compares to the promises we have in God. He's our source—the only source we need. He is our protector. He is our champion. He is our provider.

I am constantly amazed at the love of God. I am completely humbled at the knowledge that He loves me! That is a revelation that becomes the very motivation and inspiration for my life. If you get nothing else out of this book, simply know that He adores you; He loves you; He's crazy about you.

He doesn't care what you've done. He doesn't care where you've been. God woke you up this morning and touched you with a finger of love, as my grandma used to say. He allowed you to see a day you've never seen before and shall never see again, for one reason and one reason only: because He loves you! He knows all you've said and thought and done during your life and He still loves you. There are people who know me, but don't love me. We all have people in their lives who know them, but don't love them. Then there are others who love me but don't truly *know* me. No doubt, you've got some of those, too. But God is so much God that He knows me and loves me anyway. I don't care what people said about you, I don't care what you've been involved in, I don't care what they called you, I don't care what you've done, I don't care what you've been, *God loves you!*

The God who loves you is the source of all of your provisions for life. The God who loves you will provide for you. And because He loves you, He releases into your life expressions of His love called *blessings*. The very essence of God is that God is love, as it says in First John 4:8. The God who is love, loves so much that He *gives*. Once you declare and acknowledge that God loves you, you must then declare and acknowledge that He is your source and that you look to nothing and to no one else but Him—not the world; not your boss; not your bank account; not the government; not your parents; not your looks; not your intelligence, your degrees, or your resume. Not anything or anyone...but God.

Jesus says, *Don't trip out!* That's my modern interpretation. He said, in Matthew 6:34: *"Do not worry about tomorrow, for tomorrow will worry about itself. Each day has enough trouble of its own"* (NIV). Don't be anxious, don't consider, don't be upset, don't fret about how you're going to make it tomorrow. Don't trip out on that. He's a perfect Father, He's not going to mess with you—He *chose* to have you. He said, in Matthew 7:9-10, *"Which of you, if his son asks for bread, will give him a stone? Or if he asks for a fish, will give him a snake?"* (NIV). God is telling us, "I'll take care of you because I'm a good Father." He just wants us to exercise extreme caution concerning our attitude toward money, riches, finances, and material possessions, because there's a devil's snare in "worshiping" those things:

> *"Take heed and beware of covetousness, for one's life does not consist in the abundance of the things he possesses." Then He spoke a parable to them, saying: "The ground of a certain rich man yielded plentifully. And he thought within himself, saying, 'What shall I do, since I have no room to store my crops?' So he said, 'I will do this: I will pull down my barns and build greater, and there I will store all my crops and my goods. And I will say to my soul, "Soul, you have many goods laid up for many years; take your ease; eat, drink, and be merry."' But God said to him, 'Fool! This night your soul will be required of you; then whose will those things be which you have provided?' So is he who lays up treasure for himself, and is not rich toward God"* (Luke 12:15-21).

We never know for sure which day will be our last one on earth. That's why it is so important that we decide as soon as possible whom we will be "rich toward," because no one can serve two masters. Either we will hate the one and love the other, or we will be devoted to the one and despise the other. You cannot serve both God and Mammon (see Matt. 6:24). After giving us this warning about the spirit-being Mammon, Jesus immediately followed it up with this comforting and powerful promise:

> *Therefore I say to you, do not worry about your life, what you will eat or what you will drink; nor about your body, what you will put on. Is not life more than food and the body more than clothing? Look at the birds of the air, for they neither sow nor reap nor gather into barns; yet your heavenly Father feeds them. Are you not of more value than they? Which of you by worrying can add one cubit to his stature? So why do you worry about clothing? Consider the lilies of the field, how they grow: they neither toil nor spin; and yet I say to you that even Solomon in all his glory was not arrayed like one of these. Now if God so clothes the grass of the field, which today is, and tomorrow is thrown into the oven, will He not much more clothe you, O you of little faith? Therefore do not worry, saying, "What shall we eat?" or "What shall we drink?" or "What shall we wear?" For after all these things the Gentiles seek. For your heavenly Father knows that you need all these things. But seek first the kingdom of God and His righteousness, and all these things shall be added to you* (Matthew 6:25-33).

God is saying that He provides even for the birds of the air and the lilies of the fields. He says that if *they* trust God, the Creator of the universe, to provide for them, then surely He can be trusted to provide for His children. It's about *faith!* We hear a lot in churches these days about *mountain-moving faith.* "Speak to the mountain, 'Mountain, *move!*'" There are a lot of people out there speaking to mountains that aren't ever going to move because God is not going to move them. Why? Because He wants to give us the strength, the ability, and the experience to *climb* some mountains. He wants to teach us patience for Him to move some mountains. Or He might want to give us the patience to go around or under or over some mountains.

Mountain-moving faith implies great big faith. But Jesus said, "Look at the sparrows." The essence of faith in God as the loving God who provides for us is seen not in the picture of the person who has enough faith to move mountains, but in the picture of the person who has the faith as a *sparrow.* Sparrows don't sit around on tree branches focusing the intense strength of their faith on a granite slab of mountain in front of them so it will move aside and reveal all of the juicy worms beneath it. No! Sparrows have "sparrow faith." Sparrow faith is simply this: the trust and the faith that we put in God as our source and our provider. That's it. It's not deep. It's not complicated. It's the picture of a bird that simply trusts its Creator to provide for its needs every minute of every day. Jesus is saying *that* is the kind of faith you and I need. A quiet, assured, knowing faith. A faith that trusts God as our complete source and provider for everything, always.

Trust. That is the essence of what God wants us to learn. America's money (the conversion of God-created wealth into the world's medium of exchange) still has printed on it the phrase *In God we trust.* Do we, *really?* Or has the currency upon which that powerful credo is printed become the focus of our trust?

Jesus stated the question best:

> *If you have not been faithful in the unrighteous mammon, who will commit to your trust the true riches?* (Luke 16:11)

Notes

ABOUT THE AUTHOR

FOR more than 25 years, Kenneth C. Ulmer, Ph.D., has been senior pastor of Faithful Central Bible Church in Los Angeles, a congregation with a membership in the five figures. In 2000, the church purchased The Great Western Forum (previous home of the Lakers professional basketball team), which the church operates as a commercial entertainment venue.

Dr. Ulmer is president of The King's College and Seminary in Los Angeles (where he is a founding board member and an adjunct professor of preaching and leadership, and also serves as the dean of The King's Oxford University Summer Program in England). He participated in the study of Ecumenical Liturgy and Worship at Magdalene College at Oxford University in England, has served as an instructor in Pastoral Ministry and Homiletics at Grace Theological Seminary, as an instructor of African-American Preaching at Fuller Theological Seminary, as an adjunct professor at Biola University (where he served on the Board of Trustees) and as an adjunct professor at Pepperdine University. He also served as a mentor in the Doctor of Ministry degree program at United Theological Seminary in Dayton, Ohio.

Dr. Ulmer received his bachelor of arts degree in Broadcasting and Music from the University of Illinois. After accepting his call to the ministry, Dr. Ulmer was ordained at Mount Moriah Missionary Baptist Church in Los Angeles, and shortly afterward founded Macedonia Bible Baptist Church in San Pedro, California. He has studied at Pepperdine University, Hebrew Union College, the

University of Judaism and Christ Church and Magdalen College at Oxford University in England. He earned a Ph.D. from Grace Graduate School of Theology, in Long Beach, California (later to become the West Coast Campus of Grace Theological Seminary), and his doctor of ministry from United Theological Seminary. He was awarded an honorary doctor of divinity degree from Southern California School of Ministry.

Dr. Ulmer was consecrated as Bishop of Christian Education of the Full Gospel Baptist Church Fellowship, where he served on the Bishops' Council. He has served on the board of directors of The Gospel Music Workshop of America, the Pastors Advisory Council to the mayor of the City of Inglewood, California, and on the board of trustees of Southern California School of Ministry. He is currently presiding bishop over Macedonia International Bible Fellowship, based in Johannesburg, South Africa, which is an association of pastors representing ministries in five African nations and the United States.

In 2007, Dr. Ulmer was the recipient of The King's College Apostelos Christou Award, which is annually presented to leaders who characterize the passion and values of the Christian faith through leadership that has notably penetrated the contemporary culture. (Past recipients of the Apostelos Christou award include: Pastor Rick Warren; John Ashcroft, former U.S. Attorney General; Martha Williamson, producer of the TV series "Touched By An Angel"; Lloyd Ogilvie, former Chaplain of the U.S. Senate; and singer/composer Michael W. Smith.)

Dr. Ulmer has written several books, including *The Champion in You* (about developing champions for God's Kingdom on earth), *A New Thing* (a reflection on the Full Gospel Baptist Movement), *Spiritually Fit to Run the Race* (a guide to godly living), *In His Image: An Intimate Reflection of God* (an update of his book, *The Anatomy of God*), and *Making Your Money Count: Why We Have It & How To Manage It*. He recently completed *Are You Talking to Me?—How to Hear God's Calm Voice in Noisy Times*; and he is currently working on *Keeping It Real: Living an Authentic Life*.

About the Ministry

Dr. Ulmer and his wife are residents of Los Angeles, California, and have been married for 30 years. They have two daughters, one son, and five grandchildren.

Visit online at www.KennethCUlmer.com.

Kenneth C. Ulmer is represented by Michael McCall, President of C.A.M. Artistic Management, which manages the literary endeavors of high-profile Christian authors around the world.

Contact: (310) 867-1441
or
McCall@CAMArtisticManagement.com

OTHER BOOKS BY KENNETH C. ULMER

Making Your Money Count

Spiritually Fit to Run the Race

A New Thing

In His Image

Are You Talking to Me?

Keeping It Real